Fight Club

Released in 1999, Fight Club is David Fincher's popular adaption of Chuck Palahniuk's cult novel, and one of the most philosophically rich films of recent years. This is the first book to explore the varied philosophical aspects of the film. Beginning with an introduction by the editor that places the film and essays in context, each chapter explores a central theme of Fight Club from a philosophical perspective. Topics discussed include:

- Fight Club, Plato's cave and Descartes' cogito
- Moral disintegration
- Identity, gender and masculinity
- Visuals and narration.

Including annotated further reading at the end of each chapter, Fight Club is essential reading for anyone interested in the film, as well as those studying philosophy and film studies.

Thomas E. Wartenberg is Professor of Philosophy at Mount Holyoke College, USA. He is author of the Routledge book Thinking on Screen: Film as Philosophy (2007), Existentialism: A Beginner's Guide (2008), and Big Ideas for Little Kids: Teaching Philosophy Through Children's Literature (2009). He is editor (with Cynthia Freeland) of Philosophy and Film (1995), also available from Routledge.

Philosophers on Film

In recent years, the use of film in teaching and doing philosophy has moved to center stage. Film is increasingly used to introduce key topics and problems in philosophy, from ethics and esthetics to epistemology, metaphysics and philosophy of mind. It is also acknowledged that some films raise important philosophical questions of their own. Yet until now, dependable resources for teachers and students of philosophy using film have remained very limited. *Philosophers on Film* answers this growing need and is the first series of its kind.

Each volume assembles a team of international contributors to explore a single film in depth, making the series ideal for classroom use. Beginning with an introduction by the editor, each specially commissioned chapter will discuss a key aspect of the film in question. Additional features include a biography of the director and suggestions for further reading.

Philosophers on Film is an ideal series for students studying philosophy and film, esthetics, and ethics, and anyone interested in the philosophical dimensions of cinema.

Available:

- *Talk to Her*, edited by A. W. Eaton
- *The Thin Red Line*, edited by David Davies
- *Memento*, edited by Andre Kania
- *Eternal Sunshine of the Spotless Mind*, edited by Christopher Grau

Forthcoming:

- *Blade Runner*, edited by Amy Coplan
- *Vertigo*, edited by Katalin Makkai

Fight Club

Edited by

Thomas E. Wartenberg

Routledge
Taylor & Francis Group

LONDON AND NEW YORK

This edition published 2012
by Routledge
2 Park Square, Milton Park, Abingdon, Oxon OX14 4RN

Simultaneously published in the USA and Canada
by Routledge
711 Third Avenue, New York, NY 10017

Routledge is an imprint of the Taylor & Francis Group, an informa business

British Library Cataloguing in Publication Data
A catalogue record for this book is available from the British Library

Library of Congress Cataloging in Publication Data
Fight club/edited by Thomas E. Wartenberg. – 1st ed.
    p. cm. – (Philosophers on film)
    Includes bibliographical references and index.
    1. Fight club (Motion picture).   I. Wartenberg, Thomas E.
PN1997.F4275F54 2011
791.43'72 – dc22   2011003029

ISBN13: 978-0-415-78188-6 (hbk)
ISBN13: 978-0-415-78189-3 (pbk)
ISBN13: 978-0-203-80800-9 (ebk)

Typeset in Joanna
by Florence Production Ltd, Stoodleigh, Devon

Contents

Illustrations

All illustrations in this volume are reproduced from *Fight Club*, Dir. David Fincher (1999)

Notes on the contributors

Nancy Bauer is Associate Professor of Philosophy at Tufts University, where she teaches courses in feminist philosophy, philosophy and film, phenomenology and existentialism, philosophy of the ordinary, and ethics. She is the author of *Simone de Beauvoir, Philosophy, and Feminism* (2001) and is presently finishing up a book called *How to Do Things with Pornography*, which is a meditation on contemporary philosophy's powers to criticize the culture from which it springs. Most of her writing is concerned in one way or another with the attenuation of philosophy's social relevance in the wake of its professionalization in the twentieth century.

Ben Caplan is Associate Professor in Philosophy at Ohio State. He works mainly in metaphysics, construed broadly to include the ontology of art. He has published several papers in the *British Journal of Aesthetics* with Carl Matheson and was once a Teen Movie Critic for the Montreal *Gazette*.

Charles Guignon is professor of philosophy at the University of South Florida in 2001, he taught at the University of Texas at Austin, Princeton University, and the University of Vermont. He is the author of *Heidegger and the Problem of Knowledge* and *On Being Authentic*, and co-author of *Re-envisioning Psychology*. In addition, he edited *The Cambridge Companion to Heidegger, The Good Life, The Existentialists,* and *Dostoevsky's "The Grand Inquisitor,"* and co-edited *Existentialism: Basic Writings* and *Richard Rorty*.

Sam Shpall is a Postdoctoral Fellow in Philosophy at the University of Southern California. He works chiefly in ethics, but he also writes on film and the philosophy of art. He received his PhD from USC in 2011.

Murray Skees is Visiting Assistant Professor at the University of North Florida. His articles have appeared in the *International Philosophical Quarterly*, *Film and Philosophy*, *Critical Horizons*, and *Philosophy and Social Criticism*. He has published on film, esthetics, digital culture, and social and political thought.

Cynthia A. Stark is Associate Professor of Philosophy at the University of Utah. She works on political philosophy, ethical theory, feminist philosophy, and philosophy through film. Most recently she has published articles in *Hypatia*, *Metaphilosophy* and *Politics*, *Philosophy and Economics*.

Thomas E. Wartenberg is Professor of Philosophy at Mount Holyoke College, USA. He is the author of two books on film: *Unlikely Couples: Movie Romance as Social Criticism*, and *Thinking On Screen: Film as Philosophy* (Routledge). He has recently edited three books: *The Nature of Art*, *The Philosophy of Film: Introductory Text and Readings* (with Angela Curran), and *Thinking Through Cinema: Film as Philosophy* (with Murray Smith). His most recent publications include *Existentialism: A Beginner's Guide*, and *Big Ideas for Little Kids: Teaching Philosophy Through Children's Literature*.

George M. Wilson is Professor of Philosophy at the University of Southern California. He has written on film esthetics, theory of action, Wittgenstein on rule-following, and philosophy of language. He is the author of *Narration in Light: Studies in Cinematic Point of View*, and *The Intentionality of Human Action*.

Notes on the director and writers

David Fincher, director, was born in 1962. He made his name as the director of music videos, including some controversial ones involving Madonna. His feature film directorial debut was *Alien 3*. *Fight Club* was his fourth feature film. Since then, he has made a number of very highly regarded films, including *The Curious Case of Benjamin Button* and *The Social Network*. Fincher was nominated for Academy Awards for both of these films.

Chuck Palahniuk, author of the book upon which the film is based, was also born in 1962. *Fight Club* was his first published novel. Since then, he has published nine other works of fiction and two of non-fiction. Palahniuk, together with Dennis Widmyr, established a website, ChuckPalahniuk.net, that is still running and receives over 700,000 hits per month.

Screenwriter **Jim Uhls** was born in 1957. He is a highly successful screenwriter. *Fight Club* was his first screenplay. Others include *Jumper* (2008) and *Rex Mundi* (2009).

Acknowledgments

Thanks to Tony Bruce for pressuring me to take on this project and to Nancy Bauer who first envisioned it. Adam Johnson supervised the handling of the manuscript. Without his assistance this book would never have seen the light of day. James Gehrt and Erin Fahey helped with the screen grabs, for which I am very grateful.

An earlier version of Chapter 6 was published as "Cogito Ergo Film: Plato, Descartes, and *Fight Club*," in *Film and Philosophy: Essays on Cinema After Wittgenstein and Cavell*, edited by Rupert Read and Jerry Goodenough (Florence, KY: Palgrave Macmillan, 2005).

Chapter 1

Thomas E. Wartenberg

INTRODUCTION

IN OUR POST-9/11 WORLD, watching the final scene of *Fight Club*, in which the Narrator (Edward Norton) and Marla (Helena Bonham Carter) stand hand in hand watching the collapse of several skyscrapers as a result of a terrorist plot is uncanny. It is as if the film had anticipated the first national trauma to hit the United States in the twenty-first century: the terrorist attack planned by Al Qaeda in which hijacked planes precipitated the collapse of two buildings of the World Trade Center in New York City. It is significant that, in the film's version, these traumatic events were caused by internal terrorists, not foreign ones. Project Mayhem, an anarchist, proto-fascist men's organization that is the

Figure 1.1 Skyscrapers imploding

brainchild of Tyler Durden (Brad Pitt), aims to disrupt the U.S. financial system by blowing up the headquarters of all the major banks.

Although our retrospective viewing of this scene colors it in ways that the filmmakers could not have anticipated, this simply adds a layer to our problems in interpreting this troubling and absorbing film. For as viewers, we find ourselves repeatedly asking how we should interpret the film's portrayal of its characters' response to the alienating nature of American society. On the one hand, *Fight Club* seems to be acutely aware of problems that human beings have living in the corporate, branded world in which work no longer can be a source of meaning even for those it provides with the reward of opulent and comfortable surroundings. The film's nameless narrator (Edward Norton) finds himself unable to sleep as a result of his isolation and alienation both at work and in his personal life. On the other hand, the solution the film initially offers and that accounts for its status as a cult film – the eponymous Fight Clubs that the Narrator and Durden found – morphs into a fantastic nightmare of fascist conformity. It is difficult to find a consistent perspective in the film and in our response to it on the Fight Clubs, the underground sites – are they an intentional parody of Plato's Cave? – in which men come to beat each other and in which, as a result, they experience an authenticity that is precluded in their lives above ground. Are we attracted to the film only because we get to see Brad Pitt's beautiful sculpted body half naked on the screen? Are we caught up in its violent sado-masochistic fantasy as a way out of our (post)modern conundrum? Are there other ways of understanding this intriguing yet troubling film?

Figure 1.2 Tyler reeling from a punch

These are some of the questions that motivate the contributors to this volume to assess the film and its philosophical vision. Because most of the essays include a synopsis of the film, I won't include one here. Instead, I shall provide an introduction to each of the essays in this collection.

Many viewers of *Fight Club* have condemned the film for its celebration of male machismo masquerading as a serious critique of contemporary society. Murray Skees' target in his contribution to this volume is an interpretation that takes just such a critical view of the film. Henry Giroux is one critic who had taken the film to task for its celebration of male violence in response to the feminization of male identity, arguing that such a political stance could not be the basis for an adequate critique of the ills of contemporary capitalism.

Skees points out that, like many other of the film's detractors, Giroux simply assumes that the film presents Tyler Durden as an ideal type whose anarchic displays are ones that we are meant to accept as figuring the politics that the film endorses. But Skees argues that the film cannot be interpreted as a simple glorification of Tyler and his values. If nothing else, we need to realize that the Narrator's killing of Tyler in the film's final, climactic scene indicates the film's rejection of Tyler as a role model for contemporary males, even if many young, and some not so young, men have taken this to be the message of the film.

Skees suggests that the film provides a deeper critique of modern society than one that focuses on either gender or class, the two categories that inform Giroux's analysis. Instead, he claims that modernity itself is the object of the film's critical unmasking. To understand how the film enacts such a critique, Skees suggests that we see the film as enacting the sort of social critique put forward by Friedrich Nietzsche, the great nineteenth-century German philosopher.

Nietzsche saw his contemporary culture as one whose values had to be exposed for damaging the lives of the human beings who inhabited it. His famous slogan, "the death of God," registers the first step in his assault on the legitimacy of the values undergirding the European culture of his day. But once the previous attempts at justifying values on a transcendent basis had been exposed as illusory, Nietzsche worried that people would assume that there was no way to legitimate any standards whatsoever. Violence and anarchy would pose a threat in such a demystified world. As a result, nihilism – the denial that there are any substantive values whatsoever – represented the gravest threat in the modern world.

For this reason, Nietzsche attempted to develop an alternative source of value, one that did not depend on such an outmoded idea as God for its legitimacy. Skees refers us to Nietzsche's early work, *The Birth of Tragedy*, for an account of such a new set of values. In that work, Nietzsche interpreted culture as the result of a conflict between two different principles, the Dionysian and the Apollinian. The Dionysian was the anarchic principle that refused to accept any sort of limitation whatsoever and, according to Skees, is figured in the film by Tyler Durden. Opposed to the Dionysian is the Apollinian or order-giving principle, something present in the film through the Narrator in his pre-Tyler phase.

In *The Birth of Tragedy*, Nietzsche argued that there needed to be a renewed synthesis of the Apollinian and the Dionysian if modern culture was to survive the crisis of nihilism. Similarly, according to Skees, *Fight Club* offers us the enlightened Narrator, hand in hand with Marla, as the film's figure for such a synthesis, for the Narrator has understood that Tyler is simply a part of himself that needed to be overcome in order for him to attain a successful integration of his own sense of emptiness and Tyler's anarchic violence.

Charles Guignon begins his analysis of *Fight Club* with the admission that the film's portrayal of violence, sadism, and masochism is attractive, especially to the young male viewers who are the film's primary audience. The question he poses is how we are to understand the appeal of what ordinarily might be seen as gruesome and even horrific actions, that is, the beatings that take place in the Fight Clubs.

In order to explain this phenomenon, Guignon begins by investigating *Fight Club*'s critique of the modern "bourgeois capitalist" social order for failing to provide men with an adequate sense of identity, a meaningful conception of masculinity. Relying on the work of the philosopher and social theorist Charles Taylor, Guignon places *Fight Club* into a broader intellectual and social context that helps clarify the ground for its presentation of the quandaries facing contemporary men.

According to Guignon's presentation of Taylor's view, our modern world emerged from the hierarchic world dominant in the late middle ages. The warrior-knights of that age lived violent lives, as they fought and pillaged the villages over which they ruled. These brutal action-types were valorized in the warrior's code as what men ought to do. Over many centuries, however, the modern capitalist order emerged, with a very different set of roles for men. This new social order required men to abide by the norms of a commercial system that required men to fit into specific economic roles.

With this background, Guignon thinks we have the proper perspective for understanding the critique of the capitalist society's inability to provide men with a meaningful sense of identity that *Fight Club* embodies. The Narrator is the paradigm of what a man can aspire to achieve through this social system: he has a beautiful apartment furnished with all the "right" things and a job that pays him handsomely. But even as the film shows us the enviable aspects of the Narrator's life, it shows that society does not provide him with a meaningful sense of identity, a fact figured by his chronic insomnia.

The Fight Clubs that Tyler and the Narrator found appear to provide men with a means of recovering a meaningful sense of identity by revalorizing aspects of the pre-modern model of masculinity. These underground warriors share a number of the virtues of the knights of the late middle ages, as they risk their physical integrity in struggles of pure prestige.

The attraction of the film's portrayal of violence, then, according to Guignon, is that it provides a route for men to achieve an apparently more meaningful sense of identity than that proffered them under capitalism. But attractive as this option seems to be, the film shows it to be illusory. As the Fight Clubs morph into the tyrannical world of Project Mayhem, the film reveals the inadequacy of the violent route towards achieving an adequate model of postmodern masculinity.

Where, then, does the film finally come down in regard to bourgeois capitalist society and its ability to offer individuals paths to develop identities that are authentic? Are we left with a nihilistic sense that there are no good options for developing an identity that can be experienced as authentic that do not involve the sort of violence the film clearly views negatively? At the end of his paper, Guignon suggests that we need to turn to Marla for a more positive mode of identity formation than that which any of the male characters experience. Because of the women's movement, he asserts, Marla is in a better position to develop an authentic identity than the Narrator or other men.

Cynthia Stark's chapter begins where Guignon's leaves off: focusing on Marla. Concentrating on her predicament as a woman in the fictional world of the film, Stark presents a feminist critique of the film. Now no one, I take it, would be surprised to find a feminist critique of the film, for it is very much a "boy's film," one in which all but one of the main characters is a man. What's interesting, however, are the grounds on which Stark offers a feminist critique of the film. Her basic claim is that the film lacks the resources for women to find a way to recover the loss of self-respect that the film sees as central to the crisis of modern society.

Stark's analysis of the film is grounded in recent philosophical theories about the nature of self-respect. Stark employs a distinction developed by Robin Dillon between *recognition* and *evaluative* self-respect. Within the Kantian ethical theory tradition, it has been a commonplace that human beings deserve respect simply in virtue of being human. This is what Stark terms recognition self-respect, for it is based on seeing oneself and others through each other's eyes. But she argues that recognition self-respect is itself grounded in one's commitment to values one deems important. Evaluative self-respect is based upon one's living up to the values that one chooses as the grounds for one's recognition self-respect.

The importance of this distinction emerges when Stark says that there are two different reasons why one could lack self-respect: a failure to have either recognition or evaluative self-respect. Take the much-discussed case of the deferential wife. She values her role as a man's helpmate and achieves self-respect by doing that role well. Are there grounds for criticizing her? Stark's claim is that we need the distinction between both types of self-respect in order to arrive at an adequate account of the failings of the deferential wife.

After a brief but insightful discussion of *Fight Club*'s self-conscious ironical stance and the difficulties that presents interpreters, Stark considers two different interpretations of the film. The first treats the film as gender neutral, so that all of the characters are shown to be alienated and the options for self-renewal are through self-punishment and dismantling the system of consumer capitalism. As Stark notes, on this interpretation Marla's plight is simply ignored, for she is not allowed a role in overcoming the alienation common to all in the world of the film.

The masculinist reading of the film emphasizes that it is men's alienation under consumer capitalism that is the focus of the film, as well as the means for men to reclaim their masculinity through belonging to fight clubs and then joining Project Mayhem. Here again, Marla presents a problem, for this reading simply leaves her out of its account.

To counter these readings, Stark proposes that the film, despite its critical focus on consumer capitalism, includes a highly conventional presentation of a woman's option for achieving self-respect, of over-coming her alienation: she must place herself in a subordinate relationship to a significant male. That is, Stark claims that, for all its trendy effects and avowed stance of social criticism, Fight Club places Marla in the highly conventional place of the deferential wife, as if that is all that women could aspire to.

George Wilson and Sam Shpall present an interpretation of Fight Club that is intended to clear up misconceptions about the film's political message. But to begin with, they focus on the unique nature of the film's visual representations.

It is clear that Fight Club is a twist film. That is, the information that viewers receive towards the end of the film – most centrally that Tyler Durden is a projection of the Narrator's warped consciousness – requires them to reinterpret everything they earlier saw. Wilson and Shpall begin their essay by considering the unique nature of what we are seeing in the pre-revelation sections of the film. Since we learn that Tyler is not real, but a creation of the Narrator's mind, the question arises as to how to understand the sequences in which he appears. They are not completely imaginary, since the events they depict did happen in the film's fictional world; yet they cannot be accurate depictions of the events in that world, for Tyler does not exist in it. How should we understand the structure of these sequences?

Relying on Wilson's earlier work on film narration, Wilson and Shpall suggest that we interpret the film as permeated with "impersonal subjectively inflected shots." The shots we see are impersonal in that we are meant to imagine that we are seeing what transpired in the world of the fiction. In this sense, they differ from what are traditionally called "subjective shots," shots that are supposed to show us not what the fictional world of the film was like but how a character experienced that world. On the other hand, most of Fight Club's shots contain aspects that are subjectively inflected, that is, that do contain features that are due to the way in which a character, usually the Narrator, experiences the world. So, for example, when Tyler and the Narrator are talking, we are presented with a scene as if it were an objective feature of the fictional world but the presence of Tyler indicates that this aspect of the scene is inflected through the Narrator's consciousness.

Of course, Fight Club is a twist film in that the true nature of the scenes we are watching gets revealed only towards the end of the film. And once we reach that point in the film, we need to reevaluate what we saw earlier. But our reevaluations do not only concern questions of the reliability of what we were seeing, but how we are meant to ultimately take the film's apparent critique of the Narrator's alienation and estrangement.

Wilson and Shpall argue that our reevaluation of Tyler, the Fight Clubs, and Project Mayhem entails that we reject a view of the film as presenting the problem with the clearly troubled Narrator as due to his emasculation, as many critics and some of the authors in this volume, do. Instead, they maintain that we need to see his problem as stemming from his inability to communicate deeply and authentically with another human being. Marla thus represents both the Narrator's problem and the solution to it. Like Stark, although from a different point of view, Wilson and Shpall ague that the ending and politics of the film are more conventional than they appear, for upon understanding the thematic significance of the twist, we realize that the Narrator's problems can, indeed, be solved by the presence of a loving woman.

Nancy Bauer's discussion of *Fight Club* aims at showing that the film has genuine philosophical significance. Noting that many philosophers view films as at best having the potential to illustrate philosophical ideas in a vivid and compelling manner, Bauer argues that films can do more than this, that it is a mistake to think, as many philosophers do, that the emotional impact of films entails that they cannot rival written philosophical texts in terms of their capacity for philosophical reflection.

In making her case, Bauer relies on the view of the philosopher Stanley Cavell. In numerous books and articles, Cavell has made the case that film is an inherently philosophical medium. Bauer, like Cavell, thinks that many contemporary philosophers misunderstand the nature of philosophy, taking it to only involve the production of arguments. Bauer claims that philosophy is more about changing how we understand the world than in demonstrating the truth of specific views. She illustrates her claims with reference to *Dead Man Walking*, arguing that its true philosophical impact is the potential to change the terms in which the debate about capital punishment has taken place. It does this, according to Bauer, by foregrounding both the anonymity of those executing the punishment and also the calculating rationality by means of which the punishment is carried out.

In turning to *Fight Club*, Bauer asks us to see it as commenting on two of the central notions of Western philosophy: Plato's conception of knowledge as exemplified in his Allegory of the Cave and Descartes' skeptical argument in regard to human knowledge. In an inventive and detailed exposition of the significance of Plato's metaphor, Bauer argues that Plato presents philosophy in opposition to film, for the cave-dwellers appear to be nothing more than cinematic viewers. Bauer sees Descartes' skepticism as related to Plato's because, in making his argument that none of our ideas might actually reflect the nature of the real world, Descartes reasons as if he were nothing more than a dweller in Plato's Cave.

Bauer claims that Fight Club presents Tyler Durden as nothing other than the essence of Cartesianism. This is because his appearance in the film is paradoxical: on the one hand, we need to believe in his existence in order to experience the film; on the other hand, what the film shows us is that he is not real. Because Durden is the mastermind – at least, so we believe for most of the film – behind both the Fight Clubs and Project Mayhem, the film shows that Cartesianism is essentially a pathological form of narcissism. As a result, the film transforms our understanding of Cartesianism and its errors by showing it to be caused by an ethical, rather than an epistemological failing.

In a fundamentally different interpretation of the film than those put forward by Stark and Wilson and Shpall, Bauer argues that the positive outcome of the film is registered in its presentation of the Narrator and Marla at the end of the film. Earlier in her chapter, in an unusual interpretation of something other interpreters overlook – the film's phantasmagorical opening shot – Bauer claimed that Fight Club posed the question of what the right distance was for one person to be able to acknowledge the existence of another. She finds the film answering that question in its final scene, when the Narrator and Marla, standing before plate glass windows on the top floor of a skyscraper, hold hands as they watch all the major buildings in their view implode in the culmination of Project Mayhem's terrorism. What Bauer suggests is that the Narrator and Marla are to be seen as themselves viewers of a film and that it is in that very situation that we are able to acknowledge the existence of another human being and overcome skepticism.

Our appreciation of a work of art depends upon understanding the type of work it is. Some modernist works of art are constructed to illustrate this, among other points. Consider John Cage's infamous work, 4' 33". This work is performed in a concert hall with a single piano onstage. A person, presumably the pianist, walks up to the piano, lifts the cover to reveal the keys, and . . . just sits there. He may close the cover to indicate the end of a "movement," but after 4 minutes and 33 seconds or so, he closes the cover to the piano keys, stands, bows to the audience, as if in response to their applause, and leaves the stage.

Can we appreciate this work as a musical work even though no music seems to have been played or heard? Some philosophers have argued that the work is better appreciated when it is viewed as a performance piece, something akin to theater, that reveals the nature of our expectations of a concert performance. But whatever we think, it seems clear that 4' 33" shows the relevance for the appreciation of works of art of our understanding of the type or genre the work belongs to.

In his discussion of Fight Club, Ben Caplan poses just this question in regard to the film: what genre does this film belong to? Caplan's answer is clear. We should regard Fight Club as a romantic comedy in part because doing so allows us to see various features of the films in a positive rather than a negative light. So in order for us to really appreciate the film, Caplan argues, we need to see it as a romantic comedy.

On the face of it, this is a difficult position to justify. After all, Fight Club is filled with violence. And, for the most part, the relationship between Marla and the Narrator or even between Marla and Tyler is hardly the paradigm of a positive romantic relationship, with its violence and conflict. On what grounds could one possibly claim that this film is a romantic comedy?

To make his case, Caplan looks at, among other things, the standard plot structure common to romantic comedies. As he points out, this structure involves a central misunderstanding that threatens the existence of the couple. At the end of the film, this misunderstanding is cleared up and the couple is able to (re)unite.

Hard as it may be to see this at first, Fight Club's plot embodies this structure. It certainly is true that Marla and the Narrator emerge at the end of the film as a typical romantic couple, as a number of the contributors to this volume have pointed out. But the sort of misunderstanding involved in Fight Club is far more bizarre than that of a typical romantic comedy like Sleepless in Seattle. Nonetheless, Caplan points out that the type of misunderstanding at issue – that Tyler Durden and the Narrator are one and the same person – only means that Fight Club is giving a new twist to the structure of this genre.

But what about all the urban terrorism? Doesn't the presence of that undermine the claim that the film is a romantic comedy? Caplan comes up with an interesting interpretation of the film in order to justify his claim, namely that, as the Narrator says, everything is about Marla. That is, Caplan suggests that we see both the Fight Clubs and Project Mayhem as elements in the Narrator's (unconscious) strategy to win Marla for himself.

Surprising as Caplan's contentions may be to a viewer troubled by the film's violent imagery, Caplan argues that his claims about the film's genre help us appreciate the film and value it more highly than we would if we take it to belong to some other genre, such as that of the dark comedy. And his interpretation of the film as showing what lengths the Narrator goes to in order to win Marla is fascinating.

The diversity of opinions about the nature of *Fight Club*, both in terms of the nature of its critical stance and its quality as a film, represented by the chapters in this book show that the film remains both intriguing and controversial for contemporary philosophers of film – as well as for young people who continue to be drawn to the film. As you read the different chapters of this book and ponder what stance the film actually takes towards consumerism, women, and violence, I hope you will recognize how complex and multi-layered this film is. Even now, over a decade after its release, *Fight Club* retains its ability to intrigue and puzzle viewers as they discover or rediscover it. Perhaps the contributions to this volume will help viewers find their way to a satisfactory understanding of this amazing and controversial film.

Chapter 2

Murray Skees

HAVE I BEEN UNDERSTOOD? – DIONYSUS VS. IKEA-BOY

THERE ARE TWO INTERPRETATIONS of David Fincher's *Fight Club* that have come to dominate our evaluation and appreciation of the film's philosophical perspective. Henry Giroux represents one dominant interpretation. He claims that in spite of its apparent subversive politics, *Fight Club* actually embraces that which it is meant to undo. We initially believe that we are getting a critique of late capitalist society, when we are in fact getting an endorsement of capitalism's structure of power and domination, just in a new, more muscular form. The film's ethos endorses a violent rage against the feminization of male identity that is brought about by consumerist culture. Thus, the status quo remains ultimately unchallenged and ultimately the same.

The other interpretation of the film is the popular reading that results in an unreflective embrace of Tyler Durden (Brad Pitt), the narrator's (Edward Norton) confident, aggressive, and hypersexual doppelganger.[1] This character seems to be an obvious simulacrum of the male figure in late capitalist society that is nevertheless openly and uncritically embraced by fans of the film as a hero to emulate. This is evidenced by – among other things – high school youths who were creating "real-life" fight clubs shortly after the film was released. Unfortunately, the adult audiences seemed to unreflectively embrace the Durden character as well, even if they didn't intend to sacrifice job security by actually creating fight clubs after work.

Related to this latter interpretation is what has struck many to be obvious existentialist undertones in the film à la Jean-Paul Sartre, Albert Camus, and Friedrich Nietzsche. Unfortunately, few critics and commentators engage in a sustained discussion of Nietzsche's philosophy and how it relates to the film. Cursory consideration of the film in light of Nietzsche's philosophy leads many to believe that Tyler Durden is the quintessential *Übermensch*, self-overcoming the "IKEA-boy" he has become. Celebrating the relentless pursuit of self-destruction ultimately leads to cathartic overcoming. Many fans as well as commentators see Tyler Durden as the unapologetic Dionysian free spirit whose *amor fati* saves the Narrator – ultimately, from himself. This type of unreflective acceptance is as problematic as Giroux's misreading where he takes the film's presentation for its prescription.

I argue in this essay that one has to go back to Nietzsche's early work on Greek tragedy to understand the film's nuanced imagery. Reviewing the key conceptions of the Apollinian and Dionysian, as they are presented in *The Birth of Tragedy*, affords one the possibility of understanding how these notions relate not just to the character of Tyler Durden, but to that of the narrator as well. One must carry these concepts of Nietzsche's further, though, into latter works such as *Thus Spoke Zarathustra* and the posthumously published *Will to Power*. Reading the characters of the film alongside these works puts one in a better position to understand the film's philosophically interesting content. The ambiguity of the characters still remains, however, which allows for the dominant interpretations explained above. But that ambiguity is essential to both Nietzsche's

Figure 2.1 The Narrator's IKEA heaven

philosophy of the will to power and his revaluation of all values as well as central themes in Fincher's *Fight Club*.

In the first section of this essay, I give an overview of the film's plot. In the next section, I review Giroux's analysis of the film in order to show its misreading and subsequent misunderstandings. The final section will show how a thorough existentialist reading of the film is accomplished through Nietzsche's revaluation of all values and the will to power alongside, as Walter Kaufman aptly puts it, "the twin visions of Apollo and Dionysus."

I am Jack's existential crisis

Fight Club opens with the camera tracking an interconnected, crisscrossed pathway – marked by occasional flashes of light, which seem like electricity. We quickly learn as we trace this pathway and exit down a gun barrel that we have just been inside the narrator's brain and have exited a pore in his forehead in order to be guided down the barrel of a gun which is currently in the narrator's mouth. Situating us initially in the narrator's head is important, for much of what we will subsequently see throughout the film, in a certain sense, only takes place there. Through a quick tracking shot – tracking the thoughts of the narrator as he discusses the situation – the camera exits the window, moves, down the building, into the parking garage, and into a van loaded with explosives. Then, we move across the street to another building with the same situation. "A theatre of mass destruction," as the narrator describes it.

The narrator explains that he hadn't slept in six months. He states that, "With insomnia, nothing's real . . . Everything's a copy, of a copy, of a copy." It is at this moment, when the shot is of an office floor in front of a copier that we see an actual flash on the screen – for just a moment. We're not even sure we saw it. But, we did. It is the first in a series of flashes within the film's narrative, in which we see an image of Tyler Durden. We are actually introduced to Tyler, for the first time, here, in a discussion about illusion and false perceptions. This is important because we will eventually see that Tyler is, in fact, an illusion. In the next shot, we follow the narrator's discussion of corporate America and its domination of modern life as the camera navigates through garbage in a wastepaper basket. Finally, we see the narrator at work, visibly

exhausted and engaged in a technical, terminolo͵
his boss over his week's work assignment. Ti
coordinator traveling around the country inves
accidents for an unnamed auto company – "a major o.
a slave to the capitalist, consumer culture, the narrator

The narrator also discusses how he too has become
IKEA nesting instinct." The shot sequence of his apartme
tracking shot in which his apartment becomes the vision of a
catalogue. As the camera spans the apartment, we see descriptio , labels,
color options, and pricing for all of the items in his apartment. The
narrator shops because he cannot sleep, and he cannot sleep, he tells a
doctor, because he is in pain, "real pain." The doctor tells him to visit a
support group for men with testicular cancer. "That's pain," the doctor
quips. And so, the narrator does. The narrator confesses, during the one-
on-one time with Bob in a group for men with testicular cancer, he finally
lets go – "lost in oblivion, dark and silent, and complete. I found
freedom. Losing all hope was freedom." Subsequently, he becomes
addicted to support groups. He finds comfort in the communities of
sufferers. Until, he meets Marla Singer (Helena Bonham Carter). He first
meets her at testicular cancer. Her lie reflects his lie and he no longer
finds comfort in the groups.

It is the narrator's relationships, or lack thereof, both with himself and
others that drive the film. We lose sight of this, however, when the
narrator finally "meets" Tyler on the airplane. The narrative's focus shifts
from the narrator to Durden as Durden comes to dominate the story and
the narrator. Durden quickly dismisses the narrator's clever quip about
"single-serving friends" and narrative turns to focus on Durden. Durden
is sexy, cocky, and charismatic, all things that the narrator is not and the
narrator is initially fascinated by this. He exchanges numbers with
Durden and in the next scene we find out the narrator's apartment has
mysteriously blown up. After he first calls Marla and then hangs up, he
calls Durden. They go out for a beer and discuss the situation. Durden
dismisses the loss of possessions and, instead, launches into a critique
about consumer lifestyle, about how things we own end up owning us.
Speaking for himself as well as his generation, Durden confesses to not
caring about poverty or crime, but about designer goods, "some guy's
name on my underwear." He then suggests that they ought to "evolve"
and stop trying to be perfect. The narrator agrees. The next scene is outside

Figure 2.2 Tyler burning the Narrator's hand

of the bar. They agree to a fight. Afterwards, they have a beer on the curb and the narrator suggests they should do that again sometime. And, they do and others join in. This is Fight Club. Embodying Tyler's motto that "Self-improvement is masturbation . . . self-destruction is the answer," the members of Fight Club engage in bloody bouts of fighting with each other. Fight Clubs begin to spring up in other cities, much to the surprise of the narrator.

Yet, Fight Club is an initial stage in a grander scheme. Tyler Durden moves Fight Club into Project Mayhem, composed of senior members of Fight Club who relinquish all possessions and ties to others, shave their head, and pronounce their allegiance to Tyler. Project Mayhem begins with random acts of vandalism, but moves to more anarchic acts of violence, such as setting fires to buildings and blowing up corporate works of art. In this last assignment, Bob is killed, shot in the back of the head by a security guard. The group blames "the pigs," the narrator blames the group. They mindlessly recite the orders and rules Tyler had given them and the narrator loses his attraction to Tyler. The narrator realizes that Tyler and his band of space monkeys have become that which they are attempting to subvert, suggesting that the twin political ideals of liberalism and fascism may, in fact, be Janus-faced. In attempting to overthrow capitalism and its liberal political structure, Tyler has become a demagogue of a paramilitary group more dangerous than the monotony and boredom of the narrator's latte-infused lifestyle. In the course of trying to stop Tyler, the narrator discovers the truth about his fragmented, bifurcated life. He is Tyler Durden. He must now stop, or at least, come to control that which he has created to save him from the IKEA-boy that he has become. This action plays out in classic Hollywood fashion, through a chase scene in which the narrator is trying to catch Durden, only to realize he is ultimately chasing himself. This brings us back to the opening scene in the high-rise, with the narrator held hostage by Durden. Yet, as the narrator talks with Durden, ultimately talking to himself, he realizes that Tyler doesn't have the gun, he does. He places the gun in his mouth and pulls the trigger. Durden collapses and disappears.

I am Jack's misplaced critique

Henry Giroux situates the film Fight Club within a neo-Marxist critique of free-market economy and corporate culture.

> Ostensibly, Fight Club offers a critique of late capitalist society and the misfortunes generated by its obsessive concern with profits, consumption, and the commercial values that underline its market-driven ethos. But Fight Club is less interested in attacking the broader material relations of power and strategies of domination and exploitation associated with neoliberal capitalism than it is in rebelling against a consumerist culture that dissolves the bonds of male sociality and puts into place an enervating notion of male identity and agency.
>
> (Giroux 2006: 206)

Giroux stresses, instead, that the film reduces the problems of capitalism to the problems of the emasculated white male. The film, consequently, launches an all-out attack on femininity exemplified by, and limited to, the consumptive fetishism of contemporary, capitalist society.

Giroux is ultimately concerned, however, with showing how the film can be read as "a form of public pedagogy that offers an opportunity to engage and understand its politics of representation as part of a broader commentary on the intersection of consumerism, masculinity, violence, politics, and gender relations" (Giroux 2006: 206). Although he concedes that texts are radically indeterminate with respect to their meaning because a text's meaning is often determined by factors not prescribed by the text itself, Giroux ultimately wants to show that his reading points to the fact that films such as Fight Club "are symptomatic of a wider symbolic and institutional culture of cynicism and senseless violence that exerts a powerful pedagogical influence on shaping the public imagination" (Giroux 2006: 207).

Jesse Kavadlo, however, challenges Giroux's reading of the film as a misogynist tirade cloaked in a critique of consumer capitalism. In the context of speaking about Chuck Palahniuk's books, one from which the film is adapted, Kavadlo admits that "on the surface, the books celebrate testosterone-drenched, wanton destruction." Yet, the book, and by extension the film, according to Kavadlo embodies "a peculiarly masculine brand of masochism." The pain of the narrator is self-inflicted because Durden and the narrator are ultimately the same person. Although I too wonder, like Kavadlo, "whether readers [and viewers] can get to the closeted moral and metaphorical significances beyond the books', readers, and even Palahnuik's own occasional macho posturing" (Kavadlo 2005: 3–6). Kavadlo wants to show that the narrative might be showing us one thing, yet ultimately telling us something else. The "moral" message of the film, at least, is ultimately ambiguous. Yet, this ambiguity is as unavoidable as it is on purpose.

Kavadlo stresses that although the character of Tyler Durden appears to be something that the narrator might want to emulate, he is ultimately not embraced by the narrator. On the face of it, Durden appears confident, aggressive, charismatic, and sexy. Yet, he is a fictional character in the fullest sense of the term. He is obviously a fictional character in a Hollywood film, yet he is also a fictional entity within the story. He is not real. Kavadlo argues that Durden has been "taken too seriously by both fans and critics alike. Durden is not a generational spokesperson; even with the fiction of Fight Club, he is a fictional character, a hallucination, another kind of a copy of a copy of a copy, his own simulacrum" (Kavadlo 2005: 8). As Tyler himself quips, "You are not your job. You're not how much money you have in the bank. You're not the car you drive. You're not the contents of your wallet. You're not your fuckin' khakis." You are also not Tyler Durden. No one is.

Yet Giroux focuses his main criticism regarding the misogyny and fascist political vision of Fight Club squarely on the actions of this character, Durden, and his band of space monkeys in Project Mayhem. It is understandable insofar as the majority of the film's narrative depicts their exploits. Giroux, however, focuses on this character's political vision as if it were viable and attractive – something that the narrator realizes to be false and dangerous even though he and this character are, in fact, the same person. Giroux, nonetheless, concludes

> Tyler cannot imagine a politics that connects to democratic move-
> ments, and is less a symbol of vision and leadership for a new
> millennium than a holdover of early-twentieth-century fascist
> ideologies that envisioned themselves as alternatives to the decadence
> and decay of the established order of things. Tyler, played by the
> Hollywood superstar Brad Pitt (a contradiction that cannot be
> overlooked), seems appropriate as the founding father of Operation
> Mayhem – a vanguardist political movement, hierarchically organized
> through rigid social relations and led by a charismatic cult leader,
> that is represented as the only enabling force to contest the very
> capitalism of which it is an outgrowth. If Jack represents the crisis
> of capitalism repackaged as the crisis of domesticated masculinity,
> Tyler represents the redemption of masculinity repackaged as the
> promise of violence in the interests of social and political anarchy.
>
> (Giroux 2006: 212)

This lengthy quotation from Giroux is illuminating because it illustrates the confusion that Giroux has regarding the social and cultural import of narrative and what subsequent interpretations follow from it. Giroux is correct to point out that the film does not offer an image of demo-cratic politics that would or could be viable as an alternative to the crisis of consumerism. The politics of Project Mayhem is the politics of rationalized violence. It is fascism. Yet, its defeat becomes the goal of the narrator after he realizes that *Fight Club* has devolved into this fascist, paramilitary group.

Moreover, Giroux's claim that Pitt playing Durden is "a contradiction that cannot be overlooked" seems condescending to even the least bright among us. Kavadlo also points out *Salon's* Andrew O'Hehir who says "there's something more than a little ludicrous about sitting in a theater while Brad Pitt preaches at you about the emptiness of materialism." It is not contradictory or ludicrous; it is comic irony deployed to support the narrative. As attractive as Durden is, played by Pitt, Durden is not real. Kavadlo points out that "we must never take Tyler literally; to do so would be madness, as it is for the narrator, or fascism, as it is for the members of Project Mayhem." Kavadlo points out that individuals like Giroux "substitute what the film and novel depict for what they ultimately prescribe" (Kavadlo 2005: 10–11). Durden and Project Mayhem are not presented as an alternative to consumer culture; they are presented as an alternative that is much, much worse.

According to Kavadlo, "A careful reader will, like the narrator, be left unconvinced by Tyler's sophistry and instead notice that only his language, exemplified by Palahniuk's pumped up, brutally funny style, is powerful. His solutions – to take the film's tag line, 'Mischief. Mayhem. Soap' – are not." Kavadlo argues that the critique of modern society and modern consumerism in *Fight Club* is a critique in which "fascism is the endgame of a capitalist system that would reduce workers to drones and all personal identification to brand names and commercial transactions" (Kavadlo 2005: 10–11). Thus, Durden's Project Mayhem is a reactionary response to the modern consumer culture, which results in the same oppressive and dominating strictures to individuality that consumer capitalism does.

Consequently, Giroux and Kavadlo agree that Tyler's solution via Project Mayhem ends up producing the same conformity and immorality which it is ostensibly trying to subvert. Filmgoers may find some things that Tyler says, although cynical, also true. His sarcasm is a humorous way to engage in some trivial truths about society. "But," as Kavadlo concludes, "like the unnamed narrator, the reader must ultimately banish him if he is to survive. He may be a part of us, but a part that must be healthily suppressed" (Kavadlo 2005: 14).

We might do better to focus on the existential meditations that occur regarding religion, economics, and politics. This is the type of analysis that Peter Matthews endorses and, I think, it is superior to the types of criticism exemplified by Giroux. According to Matthews, "To interpret *Fight Club*, as Giroux and his followers do, as a veiled conservative reaction against the contemporary identity politics of the post-feminist, late capitalist era is both simplistic and shortsighted" (Matthews 2005: 82–83). While Matthews situates his analysis in the relationship between Palahniuk's work and that of French philosopher Georges Batailles, Robert Bennett attempts to draw out the existential themes in *Fight Club* by tying it to more fundamental existential themes.

Bennett, too, stresses that we must always remember that the book as well as the film is narrated by a highly unreliable narrator and that the book "employs diverse modernist, postmodernist, and other avant-garde aesthetic strategies." Although he agrees with Giroux that the film's criticism of consumer capitalism is highly problematic, he also warns against embracing the film's social satire without properly appreciating its own self-reflexive criticism. Bennett situates the narrative within existentialism, rather than neo-Marxist or feminist cultural criticism, as Giroux would seem to have it. This is not to say, though, that the representations of gender and class identity in the film are unproblematic. It is rather to say that they are and that is part of the self-reflexive critique that the film and the novel attempt. To see the representations as problematic is the point. The unreliability of the source of the narrative alongside the bad faith of Durden should put both the viewer and the reader in a perpetual state of skepticism regarding prescriptions that the characters suggest.

Bennett sees certain scenes in the film, like the scene involving the convenience store employee, Raymond, who is threatened with death if he does not go back to school, where fear or dread exposes us to the possibility of freedom, as supporting an existentialist reading of the film as a more appropriate interpretation. I agree. The scene in which the narrator first breaks down in Bob's arms and cries shows how the support groups, Marla, and Fight Club were ultimately about isolation, anxiety, and freedom. The narrator states, "I found freedom. Losing all hope was freedom." Bennett claims that

> Within such an existentialist context, Fight Club's recurring explorations of suffering, death, nothingness, and absurdity take on very different meanings that make these themes more integral than tangential elements of the text . . . Recontextualizing Fight Club within this existentialist tradition, I believe that its recurring references to sickness and death are best understood as an exploration of how existentialist dread can help foster a more authentic sense of human freedom, such as Kierkegaard's sense of the possibility of freedom, the Sartrean for-itself, or Camus's depiction of Sisyphus's heroic response to absurdity.
>
> (Bennett 2005: 71)

Camus's heroic response to absurdity is, in fact, exactly what the narrator states that he does in order to be free. He abandons hope. Camus essentially declares that we must abandon hope in a universal moral order, forsake the notion of progress, and most importantly refuse our ultimate answers to life by searching for a transcendent source of meaning, like God.[2] "We don't need Him," as Tyler remarks.

Although Bennett claims that "Palahnuik adopts a pre-, proto-, or para-existentialist tone that resembles the work of early and marginal existential writers" (namely, Nietzsche, Rilke, and Beckett), more than more canonical existentialists like Sartre or Heidegger, he does not engage with these writers in any in-depth way. I find this problematic because to do so with someone like Nietzsche reveals valuable insights regarding the film and its philosophical perspective. Nietzsche's philosophy does offer a critical perspective regarding the film. It is the narrator that is pivotal for a Nietzschean reading of the film. In the final section of the paper, I will draw out this relationship in order to show that, although existentialist themes like fear and death are central to the film's narrative, it is Nietzsche's revaluation of all values alongside the twin vision of Apollo and Dionysus that illuminate the bifurcation of the narrator and Tyler Durden.

Have I been understood? – Dionysus vs. IKEA-boy

Friedrich Nietzsche's overarching intellectual concern was the specter of nihilism. The notion that values are ultimately baseless, that they cannot be grounded in some absolute or transcendent realm was, for Nietzsche, so great a threat as to create the ultimate crisis for humanity. According to Nietzsche

> Skepticism regarding morality is what is decisive. The end of the moral interpretation of the world, which no longer has any sanction after it has tried to escape into some beyond, leads to nihilism. "Everything lacks meaning" (the untenability of one interpretation of the world, upon which a tremendous amount of energy has been lavished, awakens the suspicion that *all* interpretations of the world are false).
>
> (Nietzsche 1967c: 7)

Such skepticism would eventually destroy all metaphysical, religious, and cultural values.

For Nietzsche, nihilism arises from the fact that, "*the highest values devaluate themselves*; 'why?' finds no answer" (Nietzsche 1967c: 9). That is, nihilism is not the result of some person or group of persons and their philosophical onslaught of scrutinizing existing values, but, instead, that the values themselves will perish due to "internal inconsistencies" (Kaufman 1974: 112). How did our morality fall into such a crisis? "God is dead!" (I am Jack's unmanaged guilt.)

According to Walter Kaufman

> Nietzsche prophetically envisages himself as a madman [in section 125 of *The Gay Science*]: to have lost God means madness; and when mankind will discover that it has lost God, universal madness will break out. This apocalyptic sense of dreadful things to come hangs over Nietzsche's thinking like a thundercloud.
>
> (Kaufman 1974: 98)

Nietzsche's declaration of the death of God is not a claim about the metaphysical status of a transcendent deity; the claim is, instead, about a social, cultural, and, moral problem in modern society. Although Nietzsche was acutely aware of how this world and the objects in it are devalued when individuals place ultimate meaning in God, he was also aware of how the loss of belief in a transcendent source of absolute meaning would inevitably drain this world of any significance.

The problem is immense. Kaufman explains that the threat of nihilism puts us in the precarious position of needing to escape nihilism without impaling ourselves on one of two horns.

> To escape nihilism – which seems involved both in asserting the existence of God and thus robbing this world of ultimate significance, and also in denying God and thus robbing everything of meaning and value – that is Nietzsche's greatest and most persistent problem.
>
> (Kaufman 1974: 101)

What was needed was a revaluation of all values. For Nietzsche, though, this does not mean a creation of new values (that time would come, though it was not Nietzsche's time).[3]

> *Revaluation of all values*: that is my formula for an act of supreme self-examination on the part of humanity, become flesh and genius in

me. It is my fate that I have to be the first *decent* human being; that I know myself to stand in opposition to the mendaciousness of millennia. – I was the first to *discover* the truth by being the first to experience lies as lies – smelling them out. – My genius is in my nostrils.

(Nietzsche 1967a: 326)

Rightly recognizing the "touch of madness in the uninhibited hyperbole," Kaufman nevertheless points out that "the 'revaluation' is essentially 'a courageous becoming conscious' (*Will to Power* 1007); in other words, the diagnosis itself is the revaluation" (Kaufman 1974: 111). The revaluation of values was an internal critique of existing values – which had, in turn, overturned previous ancient values. The revaluation of all values is a critique of existing contemporary social, religious, and cultural values.

Fight Club is essentially implicated in this task, regardless of its success. The fact that such a film grapples with nihilism is part of what Nietzsche stated would be "the history of the next two centuries" (Nietzsche 1967c: 3). The film is best described not as a critique of late capitalist society, but rather as a critique of modernity, exposing the more general existential crisis occurring in religion, economics, and politics. Nietzsche is right to call this "nihilism." Its epicenter is much deeper than a crisis in class or gender relations.[4] Thus, Giroux's criticism regarding the film's inability to get at the roots of class conflict in late capitalist society is misplaced because the root cause of the narrator's crisis and his subsequent creation of Durden are different than what Giroux assumes. Moreover, where Giroux wants an engaged political commentary, Matthews is right to point out that such an engagement is impossible and useless. The film is as much a critique of democratic liberalism as it is totalitarian fascism. The reason is that both ideologies are caught up in a crisis of values that begins with the Enlightenment, even though the criticism in the film focuses attention on the corporate culture of consumption.

Such a revaluation, though, is ultimately a war against one's self. The accepted values are both society's values and also the individual's. Revaluating one's values is a dreadful task, a dangerous task, and a self-destructive task. Only someone powerful enough, or in Nietzsche's words "healthy" enough, can withstand such treatment. The one that can withstand much disease is the one we can consider powerful, healthy. Yet, to those still wedded to the "old tablets," as Nietzsche sometimes refers to them, this individual would appear unhealthy.

It is important to note, then, the type of individual the narrator is at the beginning of Fight Club. He is obviously beyond boredom and malaise. He is schizoid – profoundly lonely, uninterested in any personal relationships which extend beyond the duration of a flight from Phoenix to Philadelphia. He, instead, finds comfort in his comforter, completion in his complete set of "glass dishes with tiny bubbles and imperfections, proof that they were crafted by the honest, simple, hard-working, indigenous peoples of – wherever." IKEA-boy is the devotee of the designer brand. Meaning is found in determining what type of dining set defines him as a person. Purchasing – the only true categorical imperative left – becomes the penance we must pay to receive the reward of individualized value and worth. Yet, these values are empty, as Nietzsche memorably illustrated in Twilight of the Idols when false gods are made to ring hollow once struck with the philosopher's hammer.

If the film, then, is better understood in terms of proto-existential themes like Nietzsche's death of God thesis and the need for a revaluation of all values, how can this revaluation be accomplished and by whom? What sort of free spirit would be up to the task? What must the narrator become if he is to "overcome" his existential crisis? For the answer to this question, we must first look to Nietzsche's early work on Greek tragedy and his conceptions of the Apollinian and Dionysian.[5]

Nietzsche claims that The Birth of Tragedy might have been better titled, "Hellenism and Pessimism," "suggesting the first instruction about how the Greeks got over their pessimism, how they overcame it." The main theses of the book are the discovery and subsequent explanation of the Dionysian phenomenon in Greek culture and the claim of Socrates as an example of decadence (Nietzsche 1967b: 270–71).

I will focus on the former. Contrary to the inclination to devalue this world in favor of some transcendent world (evident in the ideologies of Christianity, German Idealism, and even Plato), Nietzsche speaks of the attitude in Greek culture to affirm this life.

> Saying Yes to life even in its strangest and hardest problems; the will to life rejoicing over its own inexhaustibility even in the very sacrifice of its highest types – that is what I called Dionysian, that is

what I understood as the bridge to the psychology of the tragic poet. Not in order to get rid of terror and pity, not in order to purge oneself of a dangerous affect by its vehement discharge . . . but in order to be oneself the eternal joy of becoming, beyond all terror and pity – that joy which includes even joy in destroying.

(from *Twilight of the Idols*, in Nietzsche 1967b: 273)

This passage from *Ecce Homo* discusses the Yes-saying impulse that is the reconciliation of the Apollinian and Dionysian phenomena, which one sees synthesized in Attic tragedy.

These two principles offer ways one can view the individual but are radically opposed to one another. The Apollinian is the form-giving principle, embodied by the god of plastic energies – Apollo. The Apollinian represents classical Greek genius. It is the power to create harmonious beauty and to shape one's self. It is a form-giving force best exemplified in Greek sculpture. Dionysus, in *The Birth of Tragedy*, is the drunken frenzy that destroys all form and breaks through all limitation. It is intoxication – an overflowing, ceaseless striving. It is the ultimate abandonment one senses in music and in dance (Nietzsche 1967a: 33–38).

The birth of attic tragedy, then, is important for Nietzsche because it is in this art form that we learn the secret of the ancient Greeks – the way in which they overcame their pessimism. It is in the fusion of the two elements together, not in the sacrifice of one to the other. To sacrifice Dionysus to Apollo results in Socratic pessimism and moralism, while sacrificing the latter to the former results in "the most savage natural instincts . . . unleashed, including even that horrible mixture of sensuality and cruelty which as always seemed to me to be the real 'witches' brew'" (Nietzsche 1967a: 39). Instead, one must fuse the two principles as the tragic poet of ancient Greece achieved. Fixing the synthesis of the two impulses in the development of tragedy's chorus, Nietzsche claims that

The Greek man of culture felt himself nullified in the presence of the satiric chorus; and this is the most immediate effect of the Dionysian tragedy, that the state and society, and quite generally, the gulf between man and man give way to an overwhelming feeling of unity leading back to the very heart of nature.

(Nietzsche 1967a: 59)

Whatever the accuracy of this statement regarding the experience of tragedy on the part of the Greek man of culture, Nietzsche's point about what the synthesis of these two principles must achieve is clear. According to Kaufman, "culture is born of conflict, and the beauty of ancient Hellas must be understood in terms of a contest of two violently opposed forces . . . Only the Apollinian power of the Greeks was able to control this destructive disease, to harness the Dionysian flood, and to use it creatively" (Kaufman 1974: 129).

It is the conflict of these two phenomena first explained in Nietzsche's *Birth of Tragedy* that I believe is at work in the relationship between the narrator and Tyler Durden. Yet, it is crucial to see that Durden is not the synthesis of these two principles, but instead Dionysus unleashed without the constraint and form-giving principle of the Apollinian. It is tempting to see Durden as the fusion just as it is also tempting to read *The Birth of Tragedy* as an unapologetic championing of the drunken intoxication of Dionysus over the steady, measured creative genius of Apollo. Nietzsche seems to celebrate the former over the latter, but Kaufman stresses that, if this is so, it is only to show that the Apollinian genius of the Greeks cannot be understood apart from Dionysian frenzy.

Moreover, it must be understood that the Dionysus of *The Birth of Tragedy* is not the Dionysus of the later Nietzsche. By the late 1880s, according to Kaufman, Nietzsche had changed his use of Dionysus. Dionysus now was the *fusion* of the two forces first presented in his book on Greek tragedy. Dionysus in his later works references the controlled passions of the artist, of the creator. It is in contradistinction to the Christian extirpation of the passions and the body. This is best understood in the last line of Nietzsche's *Ecce Homo*, "Have I been understood – *Dionysus versus the Crucified*" (Kauman 1974: 128–29).

In order to further show that Durden, if understood as Dionysian destruction and frenzy, is still only a moment in the narrator's "self-overcoming" and not its culmination, I want to present yet another way to understand what is occurring within the narrator regarding the emergence of Durden. In Nietzsche's *Thus Spoke Zarathustra*, Nietzsche speaks of three metamorphoses that occur in the stages in a person's will. Nietzsche refers to these as three metamorphoses of spirit. They are that of the camel, the lion, and the child. Nietzsche describes the first stage in the development of spirit as a camel, who kneels down wanting to be "well-loaded." This is the reverent spirit that bears much on its back.

For it is a load-bearing beast. Yet, this action on the part of spirit is one of strength. For, it takes strength to carry the weight of tradition, the duty of absolute morality, and guilt of ultimate punishment (Nietzsche 1968: 137–38).

But, it is in the loneliest moment, alone in the desert, that the camel becomes the lion. "A lion who could conquer his freedom and be master in his own desert. Here, he seeks out his last master: he wants to fight him and his last god; for ultimate victory he wants to fight with the great dragon." The dragon, in turn, comes bearing the name, "Thou shalt." The spirit of the lion is strong enough to fight and to conquer absolute value – transcendent sources of rule and law. The spirit of the lion says, instead, "I will."

> To create new values – that even the lion cannot do; but the creation of freedom for oneself for new creation – that is within the power of the lion. The creation of freedom for oneself and a sacred "No" even to duty – for that, my brothers, the lion is needed. To assume the right to new values – that is the most terrifying assumption for a reverent spirit that would bear much.
>
> (Nietzsche 1968: 139)

Absolute value, transcendent meaning, even cultural norms are "Thou shalts" against which the lion rages, though even the lion is not enough to take the spirit to its final stage of metamorphosis (Nietzsche 1968: 138–39). For this, one's spirit must be like that of a child. What can a child do that a lion cannot do? "The child is innocence and forgetting, a new beginning, a game, a self-propelled wheel, a first movement, a sacred 'Yes'" (Nietzsche 1968: 139). To create new values, without the gravity of seriousness with which absolute value is burdened, one must become childlike play and newborn innocence.

It is with the aid of this metaphor that I believe we are in a better position to understand the relationship between the narrator and Tyler Durden. The narrator, in the beginning of the film, is the burden-bearing beast of social expectations, managerial protocol, and cultural conciliation. He is fully obedient to the great dragon of "Thou shalt." In the initial confrontation between the narrator and Durden, after the narrator has first been called "Tyler Durden" by one of the space monkeys, Durden confronts the narrator in a hotel room. After the narrator confesses that they are the same person, Tyler explains to him that, "You were looking for a way to change your life. You could not do this on your own. All the ways you wish you could be – that's me."

Beyond the twist that this moment provides for the film, Tyler as the narrator/the narrator as Tyler, finds its best explanation in the severe need that the narrator has to overcome that which he has become. Tyler is freedom. Tyler, himself, crudely summarizes his existence by telling the narrator, "I look like you want to look. I fuck like you want to fuck. I am smart, capable, and, most importantly, I am free in all the ways that you are not." Tyler is necessary for the creation of freedom for the narrator. Durden is capable of uttering the sacred "No" even to duty. He has the power to assume the right to new values on the part of the narrator. He is the Dionysian frenzy, unleashed upon the world, engaged in mayhem and self-destruction. Still, he is that "horrible mixture of sensuality and cruelty." For this reason, he is not the fusion of Apollo and Dionysus.

It is crucial to realize, though, that by the end of the film the narrator remains and Tyler does not. The narrator is able to overcome sickness, suffering, and fragmentation. He is able to overcome himself. It is, I believe, an illuminating albeit over-the-top Hollywood example of what Nietzsche terms self-overcoming. Consequently, it is the will to power that lies at the root of the film's narrative.

Nietzsche first speaks of the will to power in *Thus Spoke Zarathustra* in the section, "On the Thousand and One Goals." In this section, Nietzsche begins with a discussion of the many different values systems that dominated people's lives. They are indispensable; one could not live without values and principles that could preserve their way of life. Yet, upon inspection, one people's good is another people's evil. It seems to be ostensibly an argument for relativism. Yet, Nietzsche goes further by arguing that all of these codes of behavior have one thing in common insofar as each of their "tablets of good" is a "tablet of their overcomings; behold, it is the voice of their will to power" (Nietzsche 1968: 170). What is praiseworthy for a group or community, Nietzsche argues, is what seems difficult yet indispensable for them. According to Kaufman, "The will to power is thus introduced as the will to overcome *oneself*" (Kaufman 1974: 200). Nietzsche takes up this idea further in a section entitled "On Self-Overcoming." The general definition though is crystallized by what he states in "On the Thousand and One Goals." Far from relativism, Nietzsche understands morals, ethics, and – by extension – political and cultural values, to spring from a common impetus within people to overcome their own limitations and weaknesses. Kaufman points out that

> The simile of overcoming – and we must not forget that the word is metaphorical – implies the presence of two forces, one of which overcomes the other. "Self-overcoming" is conceivable and meaning-ful when the self is analyzed into two forces, such as reason and inclination. Apart from such a duality, apart from the picture of one force as overcoming and controlling another, self-overcoming seems impossible.

Thus, apart from whatever plausibility such a thesis has regarding human psychology, this metaphor seems to be a far superior way to interpret the internal conflict that is raging first silently and then violently within the narrator.

Moreover, Nietzsche's conceptions of the Apollinian and the Dionysian principles make this metaphor more illustrative when thinking of it in light of *Fight Club*. It is only the fusion of these two impulses at the end of the film, when the narrator realizes that he can overcome both Tyler and also his former "IKEA-boy" self – because he is Tyler – that we see a vivid if not violent depiction of such self-overcoming. As coldly as he calculated the formula for determining automotive recalls, the narrator reasons that if he shoots himself, he shoots Durden. The narrator's rational and logical actions now fueled by his alter-ego's passion and freedom show that the narrator has, in fact, been saved – both from the IKEA-boy he was and the rampaging proto-fascist he was becoming. The narrator becomes increasingly motivated to interfere with Project Mayhem once he realizes its misguided goals and objectives. He becomes the fusion of these two primordial powers illustrated in Nietzsche's *The Birth of Tragedy*. The narrator is now best understood as a person who has given birth to a dancing star, by first unleashing this creative spirit within him and then bringing the Dionysian frenzy under control through Apollinian reason and restraint.

I am Jack's conclusion

Contrary to Giroux's reading of *Fight Club* as not only a failed attempt at subversive politics but also an implicit endorsement of capitalism's patriarchal hierarchy, I argue that the film is successful as an existential meditation on contemporary consumer society. The film is not meant to present a neo-Marxist critique of capitalism and it could not succeed in presenting a decisive feminist critique. The reason is that the film is critical of all sides of contemporary politics. Instead, the film is better read through the lens of philosophers engaged in existential critiques of the social discontent in modern culture.

On a Nietzschean reading of the film, the narrator is the individual who has organized his chaos and passions. He has become the will to power through self-control and self-creativity. Tyler Durden is but a stage in the metamorphosis of the narrator. Durden must be understood as the metamorphosis of the narrator's spirit from that of a camel to that of the lion. To create freedom for new creating, to will the sacred No even to duty, Tyler Durden is needed. According to Nietzsche, "to assume the right to new values-that is the most terrifying assumption for a load-bearing and reverent spirit" (Nietzsche 1967a: 39). It is for this reason that the narrator is initially shocked as well as intrigued by Durden after the night of their first fight. Nietzsche reminds us that "he [the camel] once loved 'Thou-shalt' as the most sacred: now he is forced to find illusion and arbitrariness even in the most sacred things, that freedom from his love may be his prey: the lion is needed for such prey" (Nietzsche 1968: 139). Durden is the passionate spirit that creates the freedom for new creating. Yet, like the Dionysian frenzy, he is also "the most savage natural instincts . . . unleashed, including even that horrible mixture of sensuality and cruelty" (Nietzsche 1967a: 39). He cannot be praised because he is but a stage, he is only half the equation.

Durden is not the fusion of the creative frenzy of Dionysus with the measured reason and restraint of Apollo. He should not be emulated. (Alas, Durden will have his space monkeys, like Zarathustra, his apes.) We only see the fusion of the Apollinian with Dionysian energies after the confrontation between the narrator and Durden in the hotel room. Durden declares that "most importantly, I am free in all of the ways that you are not." The narrator then begins an anxious and ultimately painful reigning in of this Dionysian frenzy (Nietzsche 1967a: 39). "It's called a changeover. The movie goes on and nobody in the audience has any idea."

Durden, consequently, is not the final stage of the metamorphosis of spirit – he is not innocence, he is not a forgetting. These are the characteristics of the child and are required to create desperately needed new values. Nietzsche, however, says precious little about this stage. Possibly, this is appropriate. As Wittgenstein memorably reminds us, "whereof one cannot speak, thereof one must be silent."[6] New values are not prophesy; they are not known in advance. For it takes free spirits to create new values, from the ruins of ancient temples and broken tablets.

A final metamorphosis of spirit, though, is suggested in the film's final shot. The creation of new values, the possibility for Yes-saying and innocence, seems implicit in the final scene in which destruction is the culmination of what has occurred before. And, side by side, holding hands, Marla and the narrator gaze at a new horizon, first coming into view as the pillars of modernity collapse around them.

Notes

1   Cf. Janet Maslin, "Such a Very Long Way from Duvets to Danger," New York Times, Friday, October 1999, B14; Amy Taubin, "So Good It Hurts," Sight and Sound, November 1999, 16; Gary Crowdus, "Getting Exercised Over Fight Club," Cineaste 25(4), 2000, pp. 44–48; Susan Faludi, "It's 'Thelma and Louise' for Guys," Newsweek, October 25, 1999.
2   Cf. "Absurd Freedom," in Albert Camus's The Myth of Sisyphus.
3   Cf. Friedrich Nietzsche's Beyond Good and Evil and The Will to Power.
4   That does not make these issues unimportant or unproblematic in either Nietzsche's philosophy or Fincher's Fight Club. Yet, the fact that Nietzsche often cloaks his elitism in his misogyny does not diminish the philosophical position even if its presentation at times is unacceptable. Similarly, Fincher's portrayal of Durden's independence and charisma cloaked in violence and misogyny does not force us to take the film's presentation for its prescription.
5   Following Walter Kaufman, who in turn followed the precedent established in English with the translation of The Decline of the West, I will maintain the translation of Apollinisch as "Apollinian."
6   Seventh and final proposition of the Tractatus Logico-Philosophicus.

References

Robert Bennett. "The Death of Sisyphus: Existentialist Literature and the Cultural Logic of Chuck Palahniuk's Fight Club." Stirrings Still: The International Journal of Existential Literature, Fall/Winter 2005, 2(2).
Henry A. Giroux. "Private Satisfactions and Public Disorder: Fight Club, Patriarchy, and the Politics of Masculine Violence." America on the Edge: Henry Giroux on Politics, Culture, and Education. New York: Palgrave, 2006.

Walter Kaufman. *Nietzsche: Philosopher, Psychologist, Antichrist*. Princeton, NJ: Princeton University Press, 1974.

Jesse Kavadlo. "The Fiction of Self-destruction: Chuck Palahniuk, Closet Moralist." *Stirrings Still: The International Journal of Existential Literature*, Fall/Winter 2005, 2(2).

Peter Matthews. "Diagnosing Chuck Palahniuk's *Fight Club*." *Stirrings Still: The International Journal of Existential Literature*, Fall/Winter 2005, 2(2).

Friedrich Nietzsche. *The Birth of Tragedy*. Trans. by Walter Kaufman. New York: Vintage, 1967a.

——. *On the Genealogy of Morals & Ecce Homo*. Trans. by Walter Kaufman & R.J. Hollingdale. New York: Vintage, 1967b.

——. *The Will to Power*. Trans. by Walter Kaufman & R.J. Hollingdale. New York: Vintage, 1967c.

——. *The Portable Nietzsche*. Ed. & trans. by Walter Kaufman. New York: Penguin, 1968.

Further reading

Maurice Berger, Brian Wallis, & Simon Watson. eds. *Constructing Masculinity*. New York: Routledge, 1995. (A series of essays discussing representations of masculinity in the media and in the arts.)

Bernd Magnus & Kathleen M. Higgins. *The Cambridge Companion to Nietzsche*. Cambridge: Cambridge University Press, 1996. (A vital reference work, complete with substantial bibliography, which introduces students to the work of Friedrich Nietzsche.)

Kevin Alexander Boon. "Men and Nostalgia for Violence: Culture and Culpability in Chuck Palahniuk's *Fight Club*." *The Journal of Men's Studies*, 11(3), 2003, pp. 267–76.

Albert Camus. *The Myth of Sisyphus: and Other Essays*. New York: Vintage, 1955. (A central text in the history of existentialism.)

Stevan Cohan & Ina Rae Hark, eds. *Screening the Male: Exploring Masculinities in Hollywood Cinema*. New York: Routledge, 1993. (Investigates the representations of masculinity in Hollywood cinema.)

Susan Faludi. *Stiffed*. New York: Morrow, 1999. (A discussion of the collapse of traditional masculinity in modern society.)

Kathleen M. Higgins. *Nietzsche's "Zarathustra."* Philadelphia: Temple University Press, 1987. (A guide through, as well as evaluation of, Nietzsche's *Thus Spoke Zarathustra*.)

Walter Kaufman, ed. *Existentialism from Dostoevsky to Sartre*. New York: Penguin, 1975. (A collection of basic writings of Dostoevsky, Kierkegaard, Rilke, Kafka, Ortega, Jaspers, Heidegger, Sartre, and Camus, along with an introductory essay by Walter Kaufman.)

Bernd Magnus. "Perfectability and Attitude in Nietzsche's Übermensch." *Review of Metaphysics* 36, March 1983, pp. 633–60. (These three essays by Magnus are sustained critical investigations into two of Nietzsche's most important ideas: the will to power and the Übermensch.)

——. "Nietzsche's Philosophy in 1888: The Will to Power and the Übermensch." *Journal of the History of Philosophy*, 24(1), January 1986, pp. 79–98.

——. "Author, Writer, Text: *Will to Power*." *International Studies in Philosophy*, 22(2), 1990, pp. 49–57.

Friedrich Nietzsche. *Beyond Good and Evil*. New York: Vintage, 1966. (Nietzsche's first attempt to sum up his philosophy in systematic form, written just after *Thus Spoke Zarathustra*.)

Robert Solomon & Kathleen M. Higgins. eds. *Reading Nietzsche*. New York: Oxford University Press, 1988. (A series of essays for beginning students of Nietzsche on how to read Nietzsche.)

Bernard Yack. *The Longing for Total Revolution: Philosophic Sources of Social Discontent from Rousseau to Marx and Nietzsche*. Princeton: Princeton University Press, 1986. (Seeks to find a source as well as articulation for a profound sense of social discontent found in many philosophers and social critics, including Nietzsche.)

Chapter 3

Charles Guignon

BECOMING A MAN: *FIGHT CLUB* AND THE PROBLEM OF MASCULINE IDENTITY IN THE MODERN WORLD

1

CHUCK PALAHNIUK IS AN EXTREMELY intuitive writer. The Afterward of a recent edition of Fight Club (Palahniuk 2005) describes how the book grew out of a short story that eventually became Chapter 6 of the book, a story that was an "experiment" in undermining continuity – trying to "cut, cut, cut" – jumping "from scene to scene," with no unifying character or point to provide narrative coherence (p. 213). It is to the credit of the filmmakers who turned the book into a movie that they preserve this intuitive aspect of the original. But even though neither Palahniuk's work nor the film relies on any large-scale cerebral framework, the intuitions in the film capture some profoundly thought-provoking problems in our contemporary world. Fight Club seems to speak to something deep and strange within us, and especially within the young men who are the primary audience of the movie. The film stirs up a fascination with violence that many of us may feel, an attraction to inflicting pain and experiencing pain ourselves.[1] This dark and unsettling feeling is manifest in violent computer games, popular music, and such extreme sports as cage fighting. In bringing to light the felt need for violence and pain, the film poses an interesting question: what is the source of this seductive appeal of violence that leads people (and especially young men) to find this film so meaningful?

This first question leads to another puzzle evoked by the film. There are pervasive hints that the violence and mayhem seemingly glorified by the film are related to questions about identity, and especially male identity, in the contemporary world. The developments in the film suggest that there is something problematic and confusing about being a man in modern consumerist society. The issue of forming a male identity, central to Gender Studies programs and to a number of scholarly and popular works (see especially Mansfield 2006 and Kimmel 2008) shows how the question, "What is it to be a man?" has become pressing and troubling in our world today.

My approach at the outset will be primarily historical: following the recent work of Charles Taylor (2004, 2007), I will look at how certain developments that shaped contemporary life in the West have led to a feeling, most pronounced among men, that something deeply important is missing in today's world. What this historical inquiry shows is that there is widespread confusion about what it means to be a man in modern life.

2

Look around you for a moment and observe how things work. The world we descendants of Western civilization inhabit, like the world organized by any functioning society, is shaped by what might be called a "moral order" (Taylor 2004, Chapter 1). By this term, I mean a shared sense of what things are, of what is important as opposed to trivial, and of how people ought to act and how they for the most part do act in their everyday lives. The word "moral" here is used in the sense of the French word from which it is derived, the word *mores*, and so has a much wider scope than the word "ethical." It captures not just our agreed-upon view of what is right and wrong, but also our ordinary sense of what is proper and improper, polite and rude, fair as opposed to sleazy, in other words, it embraces the "unwritten" rules of manners, etiquette, and propriety we use for assessing our own actions as well as the behavior of others. It is important to see that the communal understanding named by the term "moral order" is generally not something we are aware of when we are doing what we do. Instead, it is part of the implicit competence that shapes our familiar activities in advance, a tacit understanding embodied in our feel for the norms and conventions governing customary

interactions. This moral or\
we are initiated into the form\
we can say that our practices\
disapproval, make manifest a shar\
becoming participants in a publi\
"normalized," as Foucault (1990) says,\
rhythms of life of our community's mora\
passim).

So we can see our day-to-day practice\
accepted moral order and we can try to make ex\
What is the moral order of our contemporary wo\
reveals that for the most part we are engaged in cc ____ties
and relationships with others that reflect an unde\ ___g of life
grounded in and growing out of the economic sphere. Our commitments
and relations are almost always modeled on contractual relationships as
those are defined by the commercial sphere of existence. What legitimates
this system is the belief that it satisfies the basic needs of humans as they
are in a "state of nature," that is, the need for a peaceful system of
production that is profitable to all the individuals concerned. In this
system of orderly production and exchange, individuals are portrayed as
driven solely by self-interest, and the function of society is seen as the
production of consumer goods that fulfill their desires. When each
individual devotes him- or herself to satisfying his or her own goals,
everyone benefits. As Adam Smith put it in *The Wealth of Nations* (1776),
the individual "neither intends to promote the public interest, nor knows
how much he is promoting it." In making decisions in the free market,
"he intends only his own gain." But in this process of individual
preference-realization, an "invisible hand" comes down and intervenes
to "promote an end which was no part of [the individual's own original]
intention." "By pursuing his own interest," Smith says, the individual
"promotes that of society more effectually than when he really intends
to promote it" (quoted in Sacks 2002 145).

The moral order we inhabit and take for granted today is envisioned
as a perfectly interlocking machine in which the self-centered action of
each individual inevitably promotes the good of all. The market provides
us with an image of a well-engineered system that runs efficiently
because each of us is pre-programmed by nature to act and respond in
specific ways. Human beings are, as we say, "cogs in a machine."

...er is made possible by a homogenization and ...re in which each individual settles into a productive ...nd enacts his or her role according to the rough scripts we ...alize as we grow up. Office workers work nine to five doing what they are paid to do; students take out loans and agree to university policies that obligate them in familiar ways; academics teach and write according to the principle of "publish or perish." When we are not at work, we are engaged in chores that presuppose the obligations and rewards built into contractual arrangements: incurring debt on credit cards, securing the services of contractors, buying products on the assumption they will function well, and so forth. Even in our marriages we enact roles that are based on the model of fulfilling obligations and receiving benefits modeled on contractual market relations: for example, we enter into a marriage with the understanding that we will stay together so long as each of us benefits from the relationship. Our moral order is justified, we assume, because it is based on the mutual *consent* of all participants. So long as we remain in our society, our implicit prior consent to the system implies we are obliged to satisfy the requirements imposed by the social contract.

Fight Club begins with an image of the modern moral order in the scenes showing the narrator's life prior to meeting Tyler Durden.[2] In these shots, the character played by Edward Norton comes across as a highly skilled participant in the modern commercial moral order. He has a white-collar job for a major automobile company, traveling the country and working up cost estimates for accidents caused by defects in the manufacturer's products. The goal is to see if settling individual cases out of court would cost less than recalling the defective vehicles to repair them. We quickly see that the job calls for the sort of cold and heartless cost/benefit calculations characteristic of the "rational choice" procedures dictated by contemporary consumerist capitalism. This job, though a step above the dead-end jobs facing most young people entering the work force today, is obviously as mind-numbing and dehumanizing as the rest.

How this occupation affects the narrator is evident. He is nameless, placeless, with no genuinely meaningful purpose or role to play in the world. He suffers from chronic insomnia and seems to feel nothing. Trying to fill the void in his life, he obsessively consumes goods idealized in advertising catalogues, trying to fill his upscale apartment with stylish furniture. With spot on accuracy, the film shows the attraction of IKEA products to young professionals: he collects trendy items as if owning certain products could validate his existence. Reflecting later on his life, he describes it as the realization of the American dream: "I had it all. Even the glass dishes with tiny bubbles and imperfections, proof that they were crafted by the honest, simple, hard-working indigenous peoples of . . . wherever."

Despite this apparent realization of the American dream, he experiences chronic insomnia and goes in to see a doctor, saying he is in pain. The doctor, immediately aware that the narrator has no idea what pain is, tells him that if he wants to see real pain he should attend some support groups designed to help people cope with terminal diseases. Finding comfort in his first meeting, he begins to be a support group addict, depending on the twelve-step modeled meetings to be able to really feel anything. On these occasions, he hugs others, voyeuristically listens to tales of misery, cries on command, engages in guided meditation, all the while trying to find a surrogate for real emotion by faking a disease. This method for gaining a sense of being alive is ruined by another poseur, Marla Singer, who attends meetings for the same reason as he does. Her presence spoils the effect, probably because it mirrors the phoniness of his own presence at the meetings, leading him back to a life of insomnia and emotional emptiness.

The narrator has no friends and not even a hint of sexuality – a lack made more lurid in the sweaty, homoerotic scene of his being smothered in Big Bob's huge "bitch tits." Encouraged to get married, he says, "I can't get married, I'm a thirty-year-old boy," and Tyler adds: "We're a generation of men raised by women. I'm wondering if another woman is really the answer we need." Marriage, like the "single-serving friendships" the narrator makes on airplanes, is nothing but a contractual relationship that has value only if it fills a need.

3

The moral order of our contemporary world is based on this sort of bourgeois consumerist system, which defines the life of the narrator. Tyler later sums it up: "We're consumers. We are products of a lifestyle obsession. Murder, crime, poverty, these things don't concern me. What concerns me are celebrity magazines, television with 500 channels, some guy's name on my underwear. Rogaine. Viagra. Olestra." A Gucci ad showing an impossibly buff man in jockey shorts tells us what men should strive to be.

But it wasn't always like this. Our contemporary bourgeois order of peaceful commercial exchange was achieved through a long march from an earlier way of life to our now familiar outlook. The late Middle Ages had a very different moral order from the one we know today. In the age of feudalism, the moral order was based on what was taken to be a natural hierarchy built into the order of things, a scheme that, for example, placed noblemen above their retainers and both above the peasants who worked on the estates or lived in small villages spread across the countryside. The nobility's higher status in the social hierarchy gave the lords and knights special entitlements, including the right to pillage and loot the peasants more or less at will. Drunk with mead, the nobles and their vassals would periodically ride down into the villages and open country taking what they wanted and indiscriminately killing and raping along the way. Their position as noblemen meant that they were held to, and held themselves to, a different morality from that of the clergy or the peasants, an ethic that Nietzsche has made known as a "master morality." The chief traits of this heroic ethic included courage, honor, fame, power, gallantry, strength, pride, mercilessness, greatness of heart, and fearlessness in the face of death. The ideal of chivalry meant that knights must have sufficient wealth to buy armaments and afford servants and must show success in tournaments, power over inferiors, and piety during crusades. (Interestingly, contrary to our modern romantic mythologizing, it never included a "code of chivalry" – the noblemen were pretty much free to make up their own codes of ethics as they went along.)

The long march to civility of the last millennium was achieved through a gradual process of domestication of the rogue noblemen of the late Middle Ages. A number of factors influenced these changes in Western European culture, including reformations within Latin Christianity. But the most notable transition was the emergence of centralized monarchies in which the noblemen, who previously had been semi-independent warlords, now owed allegiance to a sovereign king and spent much of their time in the royal court. With the centers of power shifting from feudal manors to imperial courts, the ethic of the nobles shifted from the older warrior ideal of chivalry to the new ideal of the *courtier* serving in the court, one who provides counsel to the king and seeks influence through wit, intrigue, and flattery. The taming of the nobles brought into existence the need for refinement and education, as well as the cultivation of those manners of the court that are reflected in our word "courtesy." At the same time, with the slow waning of feudalism there emerged a new mercantile class that gained power and wealth through explorations abroad and the increasingly efficient manufacture of goods at home. By the sixteenth century, the old warrior caste of the Middle Ages had for all practical purposes disappeared in most of Europe, to be replaced by the ideal of the "gentleman," a person who is skilled in the manners of courtly love, sycophantic flattery, and humanistic erudition. The transformation of the class of warrior chieftains into "a nobility of servants to the Crown/nation" (Taylor 2004 33), together with the ascendancy of the merchant class, opened the door for the idea of egalitarianism, the idea that all people are equals in the monolithic system of exchange and cooperative endeavor. These developments in civil society helped to pave the way to modern capitalism and to our modern moral order.

To most of us in the West, the emergence of a system that provides for mutual trust, promises equality of opportunity, and facilitates peaceful, cooperative enterprise would seem like an unqualified good. But in some circles there arises the feeling that something important is lost in this transition to the moral order of bourgeois exchange, some capacity for greatness or heroism that existed in earlier times and no longer has a role to play in today's world. There is a nostalgia for the virtues of the older master morality, especially among those who have read Nietzsche, together with a feeling that the contemporary way of life leads to degeneration of potentialities for power and fulfillment. The world begins to look effete, effeminate, "gender neutral" as we say today. The traits of hardy manliness that once were cultivated and admired have shriveled up and are covered over by the placid norms of the new moral regime.

The consequence is a backlash against the modern moral order that appears from different quarters. We can see signs of revolt against the existing order among subcultures such as the neo-Nazis and KKK, and we find constant escapes into violent fantasy in gansta' rap, video games, slasher movies, and reality TV. Extreme combat sports, fast and furious driving, road rage, macho displays of bravado, chest-thumping assertions of the superiority of redneck culture among politicians, motorcycle gangs, street gangs, along with the glorification of violence, racism, homophobia, and misogyny in certain popular lifestyles and artforms – all of these speak of a deep discontent with the ideal of smoothly functioning bourgeois life. Occasional paroxysms of violence, extending from scapegoating of minorities to secretive self-mutilation, suggest that what most of us regard as the highest possible achievement of civilization others regard as the appearance of Nietzsche's "last men." This discontent appears especially in certain circles of young men, where there is the sense that contemporary society emasculates men, robs them of their "manly" capacities for self-assertion, of their ethos of brotherhood, loyalty, and independence, while leveling all social existence down to a bland, dreary "playing nice." Men are no longer self-legislating centers of agency, no longer sovereign subjects whose worth as humans consists in their forcefulness, uninhibited freedom, and fearlessness.

Disaffection with the prevailing moral order can take a more radical form than occasional protests from the fringes. Harvey Mansfield (2006) describes a totalizing rejection of values that comes from what he calls "manly nihilism" (see Chapter 4).[3] According to Mansfield's story, the feeling that our peaceful, gender-neutral system of consumption and exchange has obliterated the role of masculine identity leads initially to forms of self-assertion in which men try to establish their role as centers of empowered agency by heroic actions. In the most extreme form of affirmation of power, such manly self-assertion amounts to claiming that "man is the source of all meaning," and that "nothing else has meaning unless man supplies it" (Mansfield 2004 82).

This ultimate stance of self-assertion begins from the recognition that all meanings and values in the world are created by humans through their socially coordinated ways of taking and interpreting things. The recognition that there is no other source of value than humans is the basis for Nietzsche's famous words, "God is dead" (Nietzsche 1974 §125). The point of this claim is not that religions are in decline; the statement is really not directly about religion at all. Instead, the statement that God is dead tells us that, as a result of such new scientific developments as Darwin's theory of evolution, people are coming to realize that everything formerly taken as an Absolute throughout human history – every conception of a more-than-human source of meaning and values, whether that be thought of as Nature or God or Science or Reason – that all of these are ultimately human constructs. Through this realization, people are less and less inclined to think that any Absolute is credible any longer, and it comes to appear that every claim to absolute authority has in fact been a ruse of a social system intent on legitimating its own power. Mansfield holds that, when we recognize that "human invention is left to its own devices," then "manliness is unconstrained because there is nothing outside manliness, or human assertion, to restrain it. . . . Manly assertiveness feeds on itself alone and does not serve to protect a cause greater than itself" (Mansfield 2006 83).

Nietzsche saw that this realization of the death of Absolutes could lead to a widespread defeatist attitude – the feeling we have been robbed of something we once had, with the corresponding attitude that nothing is worth doing any longer. But he also held that the death of God could lead to an "active nihilism" in which individuals "manned up" to the situation, acknowledged that there are no higher causes or goals inscribed in the heavens, and decided to take charge of their own lives, creating their own tables of values and their own world order (Nietzsche 1974 §343).

This creative stance requires that one resist the dominant order by engaging in constant transgression. But it is important to see that, after the death of God, revolt cannot be *in the name of* any cause or *for the sake of* achieving any goal. Because nihilism recognizes that all so-called "higher" values and ideals throughout history have been ploys of the ruling class designed to manipulate and dominate the masses, revolt cannot pretend to be justified by any moral stance or ideal whatsoever. If *all* ideals are products of the machinations of a dominant order, then authentic revolt cannot be for anything without being co-opted by that order. It follows, then, that there can only be revolt for the sake of revolt. Manliness is affirmed by indiscriminate acts of resistance against the moral order with no pretence of a higher aim.

4

The narrator's initial absorption in the moral order of commercial exchange begins to fall apart when he "meets" Tyler Durden on a plane during a routine flight. Landing at the airport, he finds that his apartment and all he owns has been destroyed in an explosion. With nowhere to turn, he calls Tyler and the two meet at a bar. After a few beers, Tyler offers the narrator the option of staying at his house, provided that the narrator first hit him as hard as he can. This first blow leads to a

Figure 3.1 Tyler bare chested in a fight club

prolonged, bloody fight in which both men end up battered and drained. As a consequence of this violence, the narrator's personality is visibly changed. Earlier he had whined about being in pain and sought the feeling of vicarious pain at support group meetings. When the attempt to feel something in this way failed, he was once again sleepless and devoid of feelings. But now, in experiencing intense physical pain, he was able to really feel something. The experience of being hit, striking back in rage, followed by a rain of blows – all this brings him fully into the present moment and makes him feel genuinely alive. The immediacy of powerful sensations breaks through the drab existence of endless commercial transactions. Intense pain produces a capacity for focus and intensity of experience, as seen in the incredibly painful lye burn given on the hand "with a kiss."

The fighting of the two attracts more men until there is a "fight club" in the bar's basement. The club has rules, the main ones being that you never talk about fight club. But the bare-knuckle fighting itself is pretty much unconstrained, allowing fighters to beat each other into a pulp so long as neither yells "Stop" or "goes limp." Soon men throughout the city are walking around with broken bones and fiery swellings on their faces, wearing their wounds like badges of manly courage. As a secret society, these men have retrieved the age-old ethos of the warrior, where one's identity as a self is formed by facing mortal combat. The ability to take a beating and to dish it out earns a man the recognition of equals in a world where raw power is what matters most (Hoffman 1983). And the sensation of pain defines the boundaries of the self, forming an individual into an embodied subject.

Now you can *be* someone: a warrior, a fighter, a "real man." Displays of machismo stir the blood and fan the flames of sensual pleasures. This is a world for men only: the fundamental law of the "Guy Code" of young men in America – "Bros Before Hos" (Kimmel 2008 14–15, 67) – is made concrete in the subterranean bloodfest. Men are banded together in an activity that lets them forcefully assert and intensely manifest their own being as violent, agentive males. Manliness is given concrete expression not in the desiccated "courtesy" of effete gentlemanliness, but in the form of recapturing one's being as a pre-civilized center of power and endurance, like animals fighting to be the alpha male of the pack.

The base-level blow and counter-blow of the fight clubs give young men a way to assert themselves as centers of agency. Tyler Durden carries this project of asserting his identity outside the confines of the fight club. He is hellbent on a project of subverting as much of comfortable mainstream society as possible. He works as a waiter in an exclusive restaurant in order to be able to urinate in the soup eaten by wealthy patrons. He works as a projectionist in a movie theater where he splices crude footage from old pornographic movies into the family fare being shown on the screen. He runs a profitable soap company by making soap from women's fat that is stolen from the garbage bins of liposuction clinics, soap which then is sold back to the wealthy women as a luxury item. His strategy of self-assertion involves nonstop sabotage, subversion, desecration, and transgression. In every situation, he manifests his male prerogative by running against the grain, doing the unthinkable, shattering the complacent flow of everyday existence.

Figure 3.2 A typical beating

Tyler's stance of unrelenting transgression and resistance is expanded by the formation of a community of young men who dedicate themselves to modeling the kind of self-assertion Tyler represents, the space monkeys of Paper Street. Like the crews of "buds" who inhabit "Guyland," these young men find a sense of personal identity by being "real men." With their sets of rules and identical costumes, they find a place in a community that gives them a sense of connectedness because it opposes itself to what is "other," namely, the placid, smooth-running world of the modern moral order. They inscribe their identity as self-asserting males on their bodies with shaved heads, identical scars, adherence to secret rules and ritualized combat.

As the film progresses, however, we start to suspect that this way of achieving male identity is self-defeating. In order to become a member of the Paper Street Gang, one must stand for hours outside the entrance of the soap factory enduring endless insults to one's identity, slurs such as "You're too fat" or "You're too old" or "You're too blond." The aim of this abuse is to wear down and ultimately obliterate the ego of the individual so that he turns into a nameless placeholder in the constantly expanding cabal. Young men who couldn't find themselves in the pointless occupations available to them in the modern socio-economic system now are compelled to perform completely meaningless activities forced on the group. What had started out as bizarre if somewhat amusing acts of transgression and anarchist revolt against the system now turns into the highly organized, immensely destructive acts of "Project Mayhem." Where the goal originally had been self-assertion and the free expression of the individual, what we now find is terrorism and brutal destructiveness. The nihilist rejection of large-scale ideals and goals after the death of God stipulates that the anarchism of the space monkeys cannot be regarded as being "for the sake of" any cause. At the same time, no one seems to notice the paradox that the whole enterprise, despite its anarchist pretensions, is obviously driven by neo-liberal conceptions of "anything-goes freedom" and a supposed "egalitarianism" that succeeds in forcing everyone to fit a common mold. What is obvious is that what started out as a quest for masculine identity, the concern to become a sovereign center of agency, evolves into a cult of personality and the worst conceivable sort of tyranny. Where the goal had initially been free self-expression and recognition by others as an autonomous agent, the result is totalitarianism and total self-surrender.

By the end of the film, the narrator has come to realize that the persona of Tyler Durden, seemingly a model of masculine cohesive identity, is actually a projection of his own fractured and dissociated self. The quest for a unified self, for wholeness and integrity, culminates in radical dissociative identity disorder, also called multiple personality disorder. Needing to compensate for the emptiness of his life, the narrator's psyche has formed an alter ego that is everything he is not, leading him to carry on two diametrically opposed lives side by side. But the deep split between his identity as a participant in the bourgeois moral order and his subconscious need to be a "manly" man asserting his warrior identity cannot be healed. We see that any man who tries to integrate the two aspects of the self ends up with a lacerated, split identity, which is to say no identity at all. When the narrator comes to see that he has been Tyler Durden all along, he recognizes his responsibility for the planned destruction of the city's financial center. Even though he succeeds in eliminating the Tyler Durden persona, it is too late to stop the widespread destruction he has rigged up, and the film ends with him watching the fireworks display as one skyscraper after another is blown to smithereens. Total and complete annihilation.

5

Is there any sort of positive dimension to the end of this film? Is there anything that redeems the quest for identity and integrity of the self, any answer to the questions posed by the film? Tyler speaks of "resurrection," evoking the idea of a phoenix rising from the ashes, but there is no clue as to what this would look like or why it might be better than what was there before. A number of powerful lines suggest that destroying the consumerist culture will provide men with a way of establishing an identity on the basis of something other than one's possessions. So Tyler says, for instance, that "the things you own own you," that "he who liberates me from my possessions realigns my perceptions," and that "self-improvement isn't the answer – maybe self-destruction is the answer." At the same time, he says that men will "never be complete. . . . Let's evolve, let the chips fall where they may." These are catchy one-liners that sound like rather familiar anti-establishment themes. But they don't really point to any concrete solutions for men who seek a coherent identity in modern circumstances.

It may be that the closest we come to a positive message in this film is in the figure of Marla Singer. This suggestion might appear paradoxical given that Marla seems to be such a basket case: a totally confused and chaotic personality apparently lacking any stable identity whatsoever. But Marla has a strange appeal despite her quirks. Both Chuck Palahniuk's original book and the film begin with statements to the effect that somehow all of this is about Marla. The opening pages of the book, for example, tell us that "all of this: the gun, the anarchy, the explosion is really about Marla Singer" (Palahniuk 2005 4). She appears in one way or another in almost every central scene of the film, and she always presents a sharp counterpoint to the narrator. But the respect in which she offers a meaningful alternative to the loss of identity among the men in this story is not so clear.

Perhaps we can see her in terms of the transformative events that impacted the lives of women in the last century, especially since the 1960s and 1970s. During the same period in which masculine identity was becoming more and more confused, women were feeling empowered and energized by their involvement in political activities aimed at liberating themselves from traditional roles in a patriarchal society. These political activities seem to be connected to the central role women played in the various "life-reform" movements at the turn of the century, including the Nietzsche cult in the late nineteenth century and the Jung cult of the early twentieth century.[4] From the outset, the women's movement combined two aims: liberation from the constraints of male-dominated society and a correlative concern with self-formation that would let them achieve wholeness and independence as human beings. Over the course of a century's struggle, women achieved rights traditionally accorded only to men and were able to enter occupations formerly reserved for men. In doing so, they displaced men from their position of total dominance.

Despite Marla's bizarre and seemingly co-dependent behavior, she manifests a cohesiveness and steadiness of character that goes way beyond what any man in the film displays. Where men see their problem as needing to "complete themselves" (Palahniuk 2005 54), even if that involves creating an alter to provide what is missing in the self, Marla can be seen as having already achieved a sort of completeness. She is clearly the source of her own actions, asserting herself as a unified, self-legislating agent even in her most capricious and disconcertingly random actions. When the narrator comments on her behavior, Tyler says, "At least she's trying to hit bottom." As this remark shows, she is trying to reach the core of herself, what is at rock bottom, in order to see what sort of stuff she is made of. The men in the film, by way of contrast, seem to lack any sort of core. She has the kind of focus that confronting one's own death can bring: "Marla's philosophy of life . . . is that she can die at any moment." She clearly does not need to conform to societal standards and she shows contempt for consumerist society by wearing clothes she steals from Laundromats or buys at Good Will for one dollar (and "worth every penny of it"). She is capable of deep feelings toward the melded Tyler/narrator character and is not afraid to take a stand in different situations. Ironic as it may be, this confused and chaotic character seems to be the most positive image we get of a stable identity in this serio-comic film.

Notes

1   Marines in Iraq report the immense appeal of violence, risk, and death. Mike Scotti, the Marine whose recorded impressions provide the basis for the documentary *Severe Clear*, says, "I knew people were dying out there, but to be honest I didn't give a f—k." Soldiers get high on combat: one shouts, "This is the coolest thing ever! It's raining bombs! Steel rain!" As Scotti says, "I know it's hard for some to understand: no matter how much it sucks at times, we love what we f—king do" (Baird 2010 26).
2   The fact that the narrator remains nameless throughout the movie itself says something about identity (or lack thereof) in the modern world.
3   Mansfield 2006 Chapter 4. To speak of "manly nihilism" is not to say that nihilism is only an issue for men. Chapter 5 of Mansfield's book is titled "Womanly Nihilism."
4   The Nietzsche cult is described by Young (2010) and the Jung cult (together with a comparison to the Nietzsche cult) by Noll (1994). The predominance of women in both cults is striking.

References

Baird, J. (2010) The moral weight of war: Marines deserve to know the truth, *Newsweek*, April 25: 26.

Dreyfus, H. L. (1991) *Being-in-the-world: A Commentary on Heidegger's* Being and Time, *Division I*, Cambridge, MA: MIT Press.

Fukuyama, F. (1995) *Trust: The Social Virtues and the Creation of Prosperity*, New York: Free Press Paperbacks.

Hoffman, P. (1983) *The Human Self and the Life and Death Struggle*, Gainesville, FL: University Presses of Florida.

Kimmel, M. (2008) *Guyland: The Perilous World Where Boys Become Men*, New York: HarperCollins.

Mansfield, H. C. (2006) *Manliness*, New Haven, CT: Yale University Press.

Nietzsche, F. (1974) *The Gay Science*, trans. W. Kaufmann, New York: Vintage Books.

Noll, R. (1994) *The Jung Cult: Origins of a Charismatic Movement*, New York: Free Press Paperbacks.

Palahniuk, C. (2005) *Fight Club*, New York: W. W. Norton & Company.

Sacks, J. (2002) *The Dignity of Difference: How to Avoid the Clash of Civilizations*, London: Continuum.

Taylor, C. (2004) *Modern Social Imaginaries*, Durham, NC: Duke University Press.

——(2007) *A Secular Age*, Cambridge, MA: Harvard University Press.

Young, J. (2010) *Friedrich Nietzsche: A Philosophical Biography*, Cambridge: Cambridge University Press.

Further readings

Chabon, Michael (2010) *Manhood for Amateurs*, New York: Harper Perennial.

Faludi, Susan (2000) *Stiffed: The Betrayal of the American Man*, New York: Harper Perennial.

Foucault, Michel (1990) *The History of Sexuality—Volume I: An Introduction*, trans. R. Hurley, New York: Vintage Books.

Garcia, Guy (2009) *The Decline of Men: How the American Male Is Getting Axed, Giving Up, and Flipping Off His Future*, New York: Harper.

Guignon, Charles and Kevin Aho (2009) "Introduction" to Dostoevsky's "*Notes from the Underground*", Cambridge, MA: Hackett Publishing.

Kimmel, Michael (2009) *Guyland: The Perilous World Where Boys Become Men*, New York: Harper Paperbacks.

Mansfield, Harvey (2007) *Manliness*, New Haven, CT: Yale University Press.

Palahniuk, Chuck (1996, new edn 2005) *Fight Club*, New York: Norton.

Taylor, Charles (2004) *Modern Social Imaginaries*, Durham, NC: Duke University Press.

—— (2007) *A Secular Age*, Cambridge, MA: Harvard University Press.

Tiger, Lionel (2000) *The Decline of Males: The First Look at an Unexpected New World for Men and Women*, New York: St. Martin's Press.

Williams, Joan C. (2010) *Re-shaping the Work-Family Debate: Why Men and Class Matter*, Cambridge, MA: Harvard University Press.

Chapter 4

Cynthia A. Stark

THERE'S SOMETHING ABOUT MARLA: *FIGHT CLUB* AND THE ENGENDERING OF SELF-RESPECT*

> Excess ain't rebellion.
> You're drinking what they're selling.
> Your self-destruction doesn't hurt them.
> Your chaos won't convert them.
> They're so happy to rebuild it.
> You'll never really kill it.
> Yeah, excess ain't rebellion.
> You're drinking what they're selling.
>
> Cake
> *Motorcade of Generosity* (1994)
> "Rock'n'Roll Lifestyle"

FIGHT CLUB'S PROTAGONIST is a nameless male narrator (Edward Norton) who works in an unremarkable office building in an anonymous city for an unidentified auto manufacturer. He lives in a bland high-rise condominium, which he has meticulously appointed with IKEA furniture. He is employed as a "recall coordinator," so he spends much of his time flying around the country investigating car accidents involving cars manufactured by his employer. The narrator has become so forlorn over the pointlessness of his existence that he develops chronic insomnia.

Soon he finds himself at a support group for victims of testicular cancer. There he finds solace in "letting go." He becomes addicted to similar

Figure 4.1 The narrator hugging Bob

support groups and attends them regularly, pretending to be afflicted with the appropriate fatal disease. His insomnia disappears. And then a woman called Marla (Helena Bonham Carter) begins showing up at these meetings. It is clear that Marla is also a "tourist" and the narrator finds that he cannot cry in the presence of another faker. His insomnia returns.

Fortunately, the narrator encounters a savior in the charismatic persona of Tyler Durden (Brad Pitt). As Durden's apprentice, the narrator learns how to recover a sense of meaning and self-worth by rebelling against the system responsible for the hollowness of his existence. This rebellion consists, at first, in forming fight clubs where men can reject society's domesticating norms and regain their masculinity and sense of purpose by beating and being beaten by other men. In the meantime, much to the narrator's disgust, Tyler and Marla take up a sexual relationship.

Eventually the rebellion develops into Project Mayhem. The fighters become uniformed, tightly controlled, almost worshipful lackeys who mindlessly carry out Durden's plans for destroying society. As the film unfolds to depict the evolution of the rebellion, we see the narrator become increasingly uneasy with the aims of Project Mayhem. Then we learn that Tyler is in fact the narrator's alter ego and that, thanks to Tyler (and therefore to the narrator himself), the corporate headquarters of several major credit card companies are about to blow up. The film ends with the narrator destroying Tyler (by shooting himself in the mouth) and with the narrator and Marla holding hands as they watch the bombed buildings crumble to the ground.

Fight Club is both all about Marla and not about Marla at all. The narrator tells us at the beginning of the film, ". . . all of this—the gun, the bombs, the revolution—has something to do with a girl named Marla Singer." Marla, we learn, as the film progresses, is the impetus for the arrival of Tyler Durden, and hence for the formation of the fight clubs and the inception of Project Mayhem. She is the impetus, then, for the mission of self-repudiation, self-reclamation, and social change informing the fight clubs and Project Mayhem. Marla is the force behind the narrator's efforts to salvage his self-respect.

At the same time, Marla is, as a woman, excluded—indeed *shielded*—from this mission of self-renewal. She is, therefore, denied public and communal avenues for self-reclamation and she is denied opportunities for initiating the social change necessary for such reclamation. Her self-renewal must be a solitary pursuit performed in the margins of male-initiated social upheaval. Her only option, within the terms of the film's logic, I will argue, is to define her worth derivatively, by association with the narrator. *Fight Club*, then, despite its somewhat self-effacing attitude about the rejuvenation of masculinity that it portrays, reinforces a familiar patriarchal story: men's sense of worth lies in their joint world-making activities. Women's sense of worth lies in their attachment to individual men who undertake these activities.

My main argument builds upon three preliminary discussions. The first is a brief outline of the contours of the concept of self-respect. The second is an analysis of the links between gender, personhood, and the grounds of self-respect. The third is an account of my approach to interpreting *Fight Club* given its many layers of irony. Drawing on these preliminary discussions, I examine two interpretations of the film's social commentary—what I call the "gender-neutral" and the "gender-specific" interpretations. I show that on both of these readings the film implies that Marla, as a woman, must regain her self-respect through an intimate relationship with the narrator.

Self-respect: the conceptual landscape

Most of us believe that self-respect is valuable. And we have some idea what it is for a person to have, to lack or to lose self-respect. Furthermore, some prominent philosophers have founded their ethical theories upon the value of self-respect.[1] And more than a few contemporary philosophers have devoted considerable effort to figuring out what self-respect is.[2] Their work shows that the notion is highly complex and multifaceted.

In order to gain some clarity about the concept of self-respect, we can consider the following puzzle. On the one hand, we tend to think that it is generally a good thing for someone to have and maintain her self-respect. We might be tempted to think, of someone who has acted in an unworthy manner, "Has she no self-respect?" In this case, we see her act as *rooted in a lack of self-respect*, and we may judge this lack to be a character flaw (even though we might not blame her for the flaw). On the other hand, though, we tend to think it is sometimes a bad thing for someone to have self-respect. We might be tempted to think, again, of someone who has acted in an unworthy manner, "How can he respect himself?" In this case, we see his conduct as *warranting a loss of self-respect*, and we may judge his failure to experience a loss of self-respect as a character flaw.

How can we hold simultaneously that all of us should respect ourselves and that some of us should not respect ourselves? How can we hold that persons should always strive to preserve their self-respect and that they should sometimes lose their self-respect? The way out of this puzzle is to recognize that there are two distinct notions of self-respect embedded in our moral discourse. Following Robin Dillon, I will use the terms "recognition self-respect" and "evaluative self-respect" to identify these two notions (Dillon 1992).[3]

Recognition self-respect

Recognition self-respect is the kind of self-respect that we tend to think all persons ought to possess and strive to preserve. Unworthy behavior, such as allowing one's rights to be trampled, is viewed as evidence of, or as constitutive of, an absence of this type of self-respect. The label "recognition self-respect" derives from the fact that the view of oneself to which it refers consists primarily in recognizing that one is a person and taking into account this fact in deliberation and action. Such recognition is not to be understood as mere acknowledgment of the fact that one is a person. It also includes recognition of the implications of this fact, namely that the status of being a person requires certain kinds of conduct toward oneself and it includes an appreciation of the moral standing one has as a person.

In the case of recognition self-respect, one's being a person relates not only to the object of one's self-respect, but also to its normative grounds. Where the object of recognition self-respect is oneself considered as a person, the normative ground of recognition self-respect is one's being a person. One's status as a person requires or entitles one to respect oneself. This notion of the proper ground of recognition self-respect allows us to make sense of the commonly held view that persons ought always to respect themselves. If it is simply in virtue of *being* persons that individuals ought to respect themselves, it follows that persons ought always to respect themselves.

In order to have a sense of what would count as respectful or disrespectful conduct toward persons considered as such, we must have some idea of what a person is. Most accounts of recognition self-respect rely upon a Kantian ideal of the person: persons are understood as autonomous, rational agents who possess a special worth grounded in their capacity for moral agency and who enjoy a status of moral equality with other persons on the basis of this special worth. Recognition respect for oneself, then, involves the proper appreciation of these features of oneself and the status they confer.

Evaluative self-respect

Evaluative self-respect is the kind of self-respect that we are sometimes supposed to lose. Where the presence of recognition self-respect prompts us to engage in worthy conduct or refrain from engaging in unworthy conduct, the presence (or absence) of evaluative self-respect depends upon conduct already undertaken. Moreover, evaluative self-respect, unlike recognition self-respect, is merited. It is something that people must earn by conforming their actions, attitudes, and so on to certain standards of worthiness. Consequently, we are not always entitled to have evaluative self-respect, and some instances of evaluative self-respect are unwarranted. Likewise, some instances of diminished evaluative self-respect are also unwarranted. One may persist in viewing oneself in a negative light as a consequence of expecting too much of oneself.

Like recognition self-respect, evaluative self-respect is typically directed toward oneself as a person. When we appraise ourselves as persons, the object of our evaluations is generally our character. For example, one who believes racism to be a defect of character might lose respect for herself upon discovering that some of her attitudes are racist. So, both recognition self-respect and evaluative self-respect may take persons, considered as such, as objects. However, the object of evaluative self-respect can be more specifically identified as one's character or even particular traits of character.

Where recognition self-respect is grounded in one's being a person, evaluative self-respect is grounded in being a *good* person; it is gained and lost, preserved and reclaimed on the basis of one's actions, attitudes, and so on that bear upon or express one's character. This understanding of the appropriate grounds of evaluative self-respects helps us make sense of the idea that evaluative self-respect is something that individuals should sometimes lose. If one acts in a way that is unworthy, he ought to disapprove of himself. He would be unjustified, in other words, in feeling completely satisfied with himself.

Relations between recognition and evaluative self-respect

Although recognition self-respect and evaluative self-respect are conceptually distinct attitudes, they are related to one another in several ways. I will discuss only one of these ways, which is important for my "diagnosis" below of the characters in *Fight Club*. A person's evaluative self-respect frequently depends upon and fluctuates with one's recognition self-respect (Dillon 1992). One has and expresses recognition self-respect, recall, by committing oneself to certain standards that are required of persons as such. Were one to realize that she had failed to meet these standards, her evaluative respect for herself might decrease; she might negatively appraise herself in light of her failure to fulfill the requirements imposed by her moral personhood. In short, it is not uncommon for one to lose her self-respect because she's failed to maintain her self-respect.

There are two kinds of cases where this connection between evaluative and recognition self-respect does not obtain. One arises from the definition of recognition self-respect and one arises from the pliability of human psychology. Consider the first type of case. If having recognition self-respect is fully to acknowledge one's standing as a person, then one can fail to respect oneself in the recognition sense merely by being ignorant. (I will discuss such a case below.) However, if one is ignorant of what's involved in comporting oneself as a person, then, if he fails to so comport himself, it follows that he will not be aware of his failure. Hence, he will not be aware that he has reason to negatively evaluate himself, and so will not impose upon himself such an evaluation.

A second reason that a decrease in evaluative self-respect may not result from a failure of recognition self-respect is because one may engage in various sorts of denial. For instance, one might deceive oneself about the nature of one's own conduct or attitudes to spare oneself the pain of seeing oneself in an unfavorable light.

As much as we might be able to lay out the conceptual and psychological relations between recognition and evaluative self-respect, an epistemological obstacle remains. When we observe in a person the self-deprecating, self-loathing or self-destructive behavior typically associated with the absence of self-respect, we cannot always know what kind of self-respect a person is lacking. A person who lacks recognition self-respect, for example, might, in Kant's words, "make himself a worm" because he fails to understand his moral equality with others (Kant 1996). Or, he might contrive to do so to benefit himself. The conduct associated with this self-attitude might include, say, publicly belittling or deprecating himself.

Now, a person who suffers from diminished *evaluative* self-respect (justifiably or not) might engage in similar behaviors. For instance, the person in the example above might be so disgusted with himself, in the end, for making himself a worm as a means to personal gain, that he exhibits self-loathing, which conduct is not externally distinguishable from his worm-like behavior. Or consider a person who is disappointed in herself for some failure of character unrelated to her recognition self-respect. She might also display self-contempt, although her recognition self-respect is fully intact. I offer these observations as a confession that the "diagnoses" of the characters in *Fight Club* I offer below are necessarily speculative. I can only hope that they are plausible.

Gender and self-respect

The account of self-respect I have presented is very much complicated by the existence of gender hierarchy.[4] And it would be incomplete without a discussion of the philosophical relations between gender and personhood. A useful way to sort through the complications introduced by gender is by discussing the case, due to Thomas Hill, of the Deferential Wife. Hill asks us to imagine her as follows:

> This is a woman who is utterly devoted to serving her husband. She buys the clothes *he* prefers, invites the guests *he* wants to entertain

and makes love whenever *he* is in the mood. She willingly moves to
a new city in order for him to have a more attractive job, counting
her own friendships and geographical preferences insignificant by
comparison. She loves her husband, but her conduct is not simply
an expression of love. She is happy, but she does not subordinate
herself as a means to happiness. She does not simply defer to her
husband in certain spheres as a trade-off for his deference in other
spheres. On the contrary, she tends not to form her own interests,
values and ideals; and when she does, she counts them as less
important than her husband's. She readily responds to appeals from
Women's Liberation that she agrees that women are mentally and
physically equal, if not superior, to men. She just believes that the
proper role for a woman is to serve her family. As a matter of fact,
much of her happiness derives from her belief that she fulfills this
role very well. No one is trampling on her rights, she says; for she
is quite glad and proud to serve her husband as she does.

(Hill 1991a: 5–6)

Hill claims that the deferential wife is *servile*, which is a trait incompatible
with self-respect. Her servility, he says, rests in her failure to understand
and properly value her moral rights—in particular, those rights, such as
the right to have a say in where they live or whom they entertain—that
bear upon her status of moral equality with her spouse. Many people are
resistant to the idea that the Deferential Wife is lacking in self-respect.[5]
An examination of one of the reasons for this resistance will reveal some
important insights about the gendered nature of self-respect.[6]

   The Deferential Wife is clearly doing what she thinks is right. Her
commitment to living her life in accordance with her values arguably shows
integrity. Moreover, many of the values she has committed to—caring for
her family, for example—are hardly morally questionable. It seems odd
to attribute such a damning character flaw as servility to a person with
these admirable qualities. However, all that is commendable about the
Deferential Wife is compatible with her uncritically subordinating herself,
qua woman, to a man, qua man. And we do not have to look far to find out
why she willingly and happily does this. The Deferential Wife accepts a
common patriarchal ideal of femininity and her pride derives from her
fulfilling this ideal. To resist attributing to the Deferential Wife a lack of
self-respect, on account of her worthy qualities is, I suggest, to resist

recognizing the way in which ideological support for gender hierarchy is wrought, in part, by idealizing the traits of those on the bottom who are compliant. Few people, I submit, would resist attributing a lack of self-worth to an exactly similar case involving a Deferential Husband.

The specific combination of commendable and regrettable qualities exhibited by the Deferential Wife exposes the nature of the links between gender, personhood and the grounds of self-respect. Though the Deferential Wife disregards, in some ways, her status as a person, she obviously does not experience a loss of evaluative self-respect on this basis. Her evaluative self-respect is intact because she has *staked* her self-worth on her status, not as a person, but as a woman. Her positive self-appraisal rests upon a long-standing male-dominant conception of woman according to which women lack the status of full personhood.

On this view, although men and women both *partake* of personhood, they partake of it differently, and this difference is, *for women*, the decisive mark of inferiority. This (supposed) natural inferiority justifies women's lower moral and social standing and their role as "helpmeet" for man (Tuana 1993).[7] Men's natural superiority, on this view, justifies their role as leaders and world-makers and their exclusion of women from these activities. Both Kant and Freud, for example, assert that women are less capable than men of morality (Freud 1964: 125–29, Kant 1960: 81). Aristotle claims that women's deliberative capacity is "without authority" and that she therefore exhibits virtue in obeying men (Aristotle 1982: 1259b: 32, 1260a: 14). And Rousseau maintains that, due to her difference from man, woman "is specially made for man's delight" (Rousseau 1979: 358).

If women are not regarded as persons to the full extent—if their "womanness" makes them lesser or defective persons—and if women uncritically accept this picture (one would assume under a more romantic description), then it follows that they would be disinclined to respect themselves as persons. Moreover, if we consider the ubiquity, reach and power of gender norms, then we would expect that women would stake their self-respect on their status as women.[8] And that is what the Deferential Wife does. Her "recognition self-respect"[9] consists in her living up to the expectations placed upon her as a woman. Her evaluative self-respect is secured by her awareness that she does this well.

Two differences between men's and women's self-respect follow from this assimilation of persons with men. First, under a system of male dominance, a woman who genuinely respects herself as a person will fail, in some regards, to live up to the norms of her gender. One cannot simultaneously act as an equal and as a subordinate. For a man, respecting oneself, in the recognition sense, as a person is compatible with living up to the norms of his gender. There is a convenient overlap between ideals of personhood and ideals of masculinity. Both persons and men should, for example, stand up for their rights, demand their due, exercise their autonomy, and so on. A man who subordinated himself to another (unnecessarily) would fail to respect himself both as a person and as a man. And, he would have grounds to lose his evaluative self-respect for both types of failure.

The second difference is this: because women are expected to take as their own aim, the support of men in their aims, and because women's opportunities for cultural production and world-making have therefore been limited, women's worth and self-worth is derivative. In the first place, a woman must be in a heterosexual union with a man in order to fulfill the expectation that she supports, or at least defers to, the man with whom she is in such a union. So she must be part of such a union in order to have the proper grounds, by patriarchal standards, for "recognition self-respect." It follows that she must be part of such a union in order for her "recognition self-respect" to be intact. Second, her evaluative self-respect, since it depends, in part, on her preserving her "recognition self-respect," will be grounded, to some extent, in her success in attaching herself, in the requisite way, to a man. Under male dominance, women's self-respect cannot be adequate in the absence of relationships with men.

Interpretive framework

Some reviewers have interpreted *Fight Club* as a straightforward satire of the consumerist mindset that has (ostensibly) gripped Americans of the late twentieth century.[10] And there are indeed moments of up-front satire in the film, for instance the send-up of support groups and of white-collar office culture. Interpretations that emphasize the satirical aspects of the film, and the social criticism embedded therein, arguably underemphasize the self-referential aspects of the film, which have been foregrounded in some scholarly treatments.[11] These self-referential moments complicate the film in two ways. First, they reveal the film's awareness of its own status as a consumer item. Second, they reveal the film's awareness of the difficulty, for a critique of consumer capitalism, of positioning itself outside of the system it criticizes.[12]

The difficulty might be described as follows: the system of consumer capitalism is nearly absolute in its control over what ideas are disseminated. Moreover, it is extremely resistant to disseminating ideas that would undermine it. So, to the extent that a critique is genuinely located outside of the system, it will receive little or no uptake. To the extent that the critique is located within the system, it will receive uptake, but only if either sanitized or insincere. If the critique is sanitized—if it is drained of its radical content or tone—then it is essentially devoid of critical force; if it is insincere, then, to avoid being simply hypocritical, it must be ironic. The film must offer its critique with a wink. Here, too, though, the critique loses force. But in this case the mere taking up of the distancing stance garners the film a kind of outsider status. The way to the outside, if one is inextricably ensconced on the inside, is to acknowledge one's location through gestures of self-mockery.

Fight Club was produced by Twentieth Century Fox, one of the six major Hollywood studios. It is a highly stylized movie featuring well-known actors Edward Norton and Helena Bonham Carter and mega-star Brad Pitt. Furthermore, it is rife with product placements, most notably Starbucks and Pepsi. It is quite apparent to the viewer then, that the film is implicated in the system it sets out to criticize. It is, itself, not only an object for consumption, but one that has various accoutrements designed to promote its own mass consumption, such as extremely popular actors and slick production. Moreover, the willingness of such mega-corporations as Starbucks and Pepsi to allow the placement of their products is a clear indication that the film's message hardly poses a threat to the future consumer capitalism.

Fight Club conveys its awareness of its own status as consumer item in a variety of ways. For instance, in one scene the narrator and Tyler are riding a bus, the inside of which is plastered with advertisements. One of the ads features a beautifully sculpted, bare-chested male model advertising Gucci clothing. The narrator says to Tyler in a derisive tone, "Is that what a man looks like?" Tyler laughs in agreement with the narrator's criticism of the ideal of male beauty perpetuated by visual media, especially advertising. Early on in the next scene of a fight club meeting, we see a shot of Brad Pitt's beautifully sculpted, bare-chested body (Ansen 1999).[13] Indeed the film contains many similar shots offering such "eye-candy." So we are given the social critique and then we are given a confession: we are shown that the film knows that it is indeed an instance of what it condemns.

Another example concerns Tyler's practice of splicing pornography—in particular, male organs—into family films. The narrator is pictured, *as a narrator*—not as part of the narrative—in the frame in which he explains to us the requirements of Tyler's job as a projectionist. Meanwhile, Tyler demonstrates his job to us by pointing to the upper corner of the frame in which he is pictured to show us the "cigarette burns" in the film—the film we are watching—that are designed to tell the projectionist when it is time to change the reel. At the very end of the film, we see a penis spliced into the film—again, the film that we are watching. These formal features show us that *Fight Club* is quite conscious of its being a film. Indeed, we see that it is conscious of being the sort of film into which Tyler might be tempted to splice pornography. Hence, this splicing represents the film's admission that it is nothing more than a big studio movie whose aim is entertainment, not genuine social critique, satirical or not.

Fight Club, then, is, in a certain respect, unstable. It offers moments of satire designed to denounce consumerism. At the same time, it frequently pulls back from its social critique in its moments of self-awareness. I think these two dimensions of the film can be treated individually. That is, I believe that the coherence of the narrative's social critique can be assessed separately from the film's position regarding its own status as critique. I will focus on the social critique—the straightforward narrative—because I believe that we can uncover in the interstices of that narrative a corroboration of certain widely accepted social norms. The extent to which the film, through its self-referential gestures, pulls back from the narrative's content turns out to be irrelevant, on my approach, to what the narrative *fails* to say. It is irrelevant to what is implied by the *gaps* in the narrative because the film can insert ironic commentary only upon what it (satirically) says, not upon what it does not say.

What I will argue is that however much of an "outsider" status *Fight Club* is able to achieve through its various layers of irony, it is in the end, along a particular dimension, utterly conventional. It reinforces, I contend, a certain patriarchal ideal of femininity through its portrayal of Marla. Just to forestall a certain misinterpretation of my view: I am not standing my argument on the open misogyny expressed by Tyler (though

I will discuss his misogyny below). This dimension of the film is clearly implicated in the film's calculated distance from its own (purportedly subversive) content. In a vernacular familiar to analytic philosophers, Tyler's misogynistic remarks are mentioned but not used. What I am interested in is the film's failure—arguably colossal, given its overt engagement with issues of self-worth—to offer a coherent account of Marla's self-contempt and need for self-renewal.

It particular, I will argue that where the film can account for Marla's lack of self-respect, it cannot account for her exclusion from the revolution and where it can account for her exclusion from the revolution, it cannot account for her lack of self-respect. The result of this incoherence in the narrative is that the film reinscribes the long-standing view, explained above, of women's sense of worth as appropriately derived from their attachment to men.

Portraits of self-destructiveness

All of the main characters in *Fight Club* are struggling with issues of self-worth. Consider, first, Marla. She is clearly short on self-respect. She attempts to kill herself. She refers to herself as "a monster" and as "infectious human waste." When she learns that a support group member she knew has died, she says, "It was the smart move on her part." Furthermore, Marla involves herself in a sexual relationship with Tyler, and in a rancorous "friendship" with the narrator, both of whom hold her (and women in general) in contempt. In one scene, for instance, when the narrator attempts to peer in on Tyler and Marla having sex, Tyler

Figure 4.2 The narrator meeting Marla

suddenly appears at the bedroom door, wearing a yellow rubber glove, and asks the narrator, "You wanna finish her off?" (The narrator declines.) In another scene, when the narrator is talking to Marla in the kitchen of the house that he shares with Tyler, Tyler commands, "Get rid of her."

Marla, it seems, must be kept at bay. She is, by Tyler's lights, a danger. Tyler says to the narrator, "She's a predator posing as a house pet." And Tyler insists that the narrator never talk about him with Marla, as though this act would weaken the bond existing between himself and the narrator. On the narrator's view, Marla is not so much a danger as an intruder. When Marla comes downstairs after her first night spent with Tyler, the narrator looks at her in horror and says, "What are you doing here? This is my house. What are you doing in my house?" Later he says to us, "She invaded my support groups, now she's invaded my home." That Marla is willing to endure the abuse that is delivered by Tyler and by the narrator (that is to say, by her lover, since, from her point of view, they are one and the same person) suggests that she lacks recognition self-respect. Her disdainful comments about herself suggest that she also suffers from diminished evaluative self-respect, perhaps, in part, because she grasps, at some level, that submitting to abuse from her lover is below her.

The narrator's lack of self-respect, like Marla's, is glaringly obvious and vividly portrayed. He has difficulty sleeping, which may indicate that he is deeply troubled by something that he has done—that he is, perhaps, filled with self-reproach. The fact that his insomnia is manageable only when he attends support groups suggests that the narrator is desperately in need of affirmation from others. He tells us that when he is at a support group meeting he is, momentarily, at the center of the universe. Apparently, being affirmed by others enables him to quiet his self-recriminations enough so that he can sleep.

Another indication that the narrator lacks self-respect is the fact that he fantasizes that the plane he is travelling on crashes. His death, presumably, would free him from his misery. We have reason to believe that his misery is caused not only from the deadening monotony of his job, but also from a persistent dissatisfaction with himself perpetrated by his commitment to the consumerist values that keep him chained to his job. Finally, the narrator's destruction of his condominium, which certainly represents a rejection of a consumerist lifestyle, can also be interpreted as a symbolic act of self-destruction. The narrator, we can surmise, wishes to destroy the person whom that condo has come to represent. And, the fact that he has, just before the condo blows up, projected a new self—Tyler—corroborates this idea that the narrator wishes to obliterate himself. The narrator, I would argue, suffers from a painful deficiency of evaluative self-respect, which is founded, at least in part, upon the knowledge (itself unacknowledged) that he lacks recognition self-respect. He knows, but has not yet come to terms with the fact, that he has so far committed himself to values that are somehow unworthy of or below him.

Tyler, of the three main characters, has the most complex set of attitudes toward himself. He is self-confident, self-assured, indeed cocky, and, unlike the narrator, forthright in his resistance to the consumerist milieu that surrounds him. He appears, therefore, to have plenty of self-respect. However, Tyler is obsessed with self-destruction, both physical and psychological, which might suggest an absence of self-respect. He says to the narrator, for example, "Self-improvement is masturbation; self-destruction. . . ." The unspoken thought here is that self-destruction is a far superior method of self-transformation than the mild, superficial and ultimately narcissistic sort of self-transformation marketed in consumerist society.

The importance, for Tyler, of physical self-destruction is shown, of course, through the fight clubs, but also in a scene where Tyler dampens the narrator's hand with a kiss and then pours lye on his hand. While the narrator is writhing in pain, Tyler launches a psychological assault, telling the narrator that he must come to terms with the fact that his own father may not have liked him and that God ("the father") may not like him. Tyler also tells the members of Project Mayhem, repeatedly, that they are as worthless as garbage. "You are the all-singing, all-dancing crap of the world," he says. And, he tells them, "We are all part of the same giant compost heap."

Clearly, Tyler is not out simply to destroy himself; he endorses self-destruction for all (or for all men) as an ideal. He sees self-destruction as the necessary means to cleansing oneself of the toxins accumulated by consumption, or, to switch metaphors, he sees it as the means of ridding oneself of the disease of consumption. Tyler, then, is similar, in a certain respect, to the Deferential Wife. He takes, *as a matter of principle*, what one might judge to be a disrespectful stance toward himself. However, Tyler takes this stance in order to be an exemplar. (He himself bears a kiss-shaped scar on his hand.) He regards such a stance as a necessary means to personal and political transformation—as a means for *reclaiming* one's self-respect. So, Tyler's dedication to self-destruction, though arguably misguided, is not plausibly construed as a lack of self-respect.

The mystery of Marla

Amidst all of this self-destructiveness, how are we to understand Marla's position within the terms of the film's social commentary? How do we make sense of the fact that Marla, like the narrator, lacks self-respect, but unlike the narrator, is denied (Tyler's version of) the means to self-redemption? Consider the gender-neutral interpretation of *Fight Club*. On this view, all of us—men and women—are subject to the travails experienced by the narrator. "Like so many others," the narrator says, "I had become a slave to the IKEA nesting instinct." He continues, "I'd flip through catalogues and wonder, 'What kind of dining set defines me as a person?'" Meaningless consumption, on this interpretation, has rendered all our lives spiritually empty; if we are at all "in the know," we feel dislocated and alienated. We do not like who we have become. Yet we are puzzled by our dissatisfaction with ourselves because we have followed the formula for fulfillment that has been prescribed to us. We sense that we have somehow failed, so we cast about for some means of relief, such as support groups or large doses of Xanax.

The system of consumer capitalism, on this reading of *Fight Club*, has deformed us as persons by intimating that what really matters about us is our ability to consume material goods. It has therefore damaged our recognition self-respect by causing us to look away from our intrinsic worth as autonomous, creative and self-creative beings and to instead stake our worth strictly on our status as consumers in a marketplace. Consumer capitalist ideology has also diminished our evaluative self-respect, on this reading, because we sense (inchoately) that we have failed to live up to some important ideal. The self-disappointment or self-contempt that accompanies this realization is compounded by the fact that we cannot quite see that our displeasure has been culturally imposed. We are led to believe that our discontentment is our own fault.

The film suggests two solutions to this problem, one personal and one political. The personal solution is self-punishment. One should get beaten up; hence the formation of fight clubs.[14] The goal, we are told, is to "hit bottom" which is a necessary precursor to individual redemption. The political solution that the film initially suggests is to dismantle the system of consumer capitalism, through guerilla tactics, and then resurrect society. (The film eventually recants this suggestion as it shows the rebellion recapitulating the very crimes of the system being rebelled against.)[15] Both the personal and the political solutions, the film implies, offer an avenue for restored self-worth. Not only will the resurrected society ensure all of us a more meaningful existence, but also the very process of identifying and addressing the problem is itself restorative.

The gender-neutral interpretation of *Fight Club* makes sense of Marla's feelings of alienation and self-contempt and her inclination toward self-destruction—she, like the narrator and the fight club members, has been psychically damaged by a consumer-oriented culture. What might be otherwise regarded as her personal problems are given a political explanation. This interpretation also makes sense of Tyler's praise for Marla as someone who is trying to hit bottom. Marla, like all of us— according to Tyler's philosophy—needs to hit bottom before she can rise above.

So, why is Marla not allowed in on the revolution? The gender-neutral interpretation cannot explain why the narrative so clearly positions Marla as an interloper. It cannot explain why the revolution must, with such determination, exclude Marla, and indeed all women. (When Marla asks the narrator why he has not been to any support groups lately, he says smugly, "I found a new one. It's for men only.") If Marla is just as much a victim of the system as the narrator, then to deny Marla the opportunity for self-reclamation that is offered to the narrator and his cohort is to imply that it is not fitting that she experience this reclamation. This idea entails either that it is not fitting for her to respect herself or that she, as a woman, is required to find some other avenue of self-respect. And indeed Marla *does* find another avenue. In the closing scene she commits herself to the narrator. She forgives him his past transgressions. She accepts his explanation that his recent conduct is attributable to its being "a very strange time" in his life and she accepts his assurances that everything will be okay. Safely ensconced in a heterosexual union, Marla can begin the process of regaining her self-respect.

Consider, now, the interpretation of *Fight Club* that identifies the narrator's predicament as a specifically masculine one.[16] On this reading, the main harm of consumer capitalism is that it emasculates and domesticates men. White-collar men, such as the narrator, are impelled to take on the narcissistic trappings of femininity, such as an abiding interest in decor. "We used to read pornography," the narrator laments, "now it was the Horchow Collection." Blue-collar men, such as Tyler, are forced to take on the support-oriented trappings of femininity through mundane service jobs such as waiter or bartender. Tyler warns the police commissioner, who has vowed to crack down on the fight clubs (and whom Tyler is at the same time threatening to castrate), "Look, the people you are after are the people you depend on. We cook your meals. We haul your trash. We connect your calls. We drive your ambulances. We guard you while you sleep. Do not fuck with us."

On the gender-specific reading, consumer society has driven men to feel empty, dislocated, alienated. It has deformed men by depriving them of contact with or experience of their masculine natures. Consumer culture, then, has damaged men's "recognition self-respect" by forcing them to embrace the feminine values of consumption and service. By lowering themselves in this way, men have diminished themselves both as men and as persons. No self-respecting man would willingly embrace the feminine; no self-respecting person would willingly ignore his status as a person in the way the embracing of the feminine requires. Consumer capitalist ideology is also an obstacle to men's evaluative self-respect, on this reading, because men sense, but do not fully grasp, that they have failed in some way to live up to some important ideals. Their feelings of worthlessness are compounded by the fact that they cannot quite see that their dissatisfaction has been imposed by a feminizing culture. They are led to believe that the source of their discontentment resides in them.

The solution to this problem, according to the gender-specific reading of Fight Club, is for men to reclaim their masculinity, and hence their status as full persons, first, by being beaten up, and second, by renovating society. Physical suffering, at the hands of other men, is the means by which men are reunited with their masculinity. They must have the femininity literally beaten out of them. Once this transformation has taken place on a large enough scale, society itself can be transformed. The new society will ensure that men remain men.[17] "In the world I see," Tyler says, "you're stalking elk through the damp canyon forest around the ruins of Rockefeller Center. You'll wear leather clothes that will last you the rest of your life.[18] You'll climb the wrist-thick kudzu vines that wrap the Sears Tower. And when you look down, you will see tiny figures[19] pounding corn and laying strips of venison in the empty carpool lane of some abandoned super-highway."

The gender-specific interpretation of *Fight Club* easily makes sense of Marla's exclusion from the revolution. As the literal and figurative embodiment of toxic femininity (hence Tyler's rubber glove), Marla is part of the problem. Though useful to Tyler as a "sport fuck," she poses a threat to men and to the success of the political transformation envisioned by Tyler. Tyler says to the narrator, "We're a generation of men raised by women; I'm wondering if another woman is really the answer we need."

The gender-specific interpretation, however, cannot make sense of Marla's self-contempt. *Marla* has not been emasculated by consumer society, or perhaps, she has, but she has not been harmed by the process; she's instead been appropriately shaped by it. So why is *Marla* joining support groups for diseases she does not have? And why is Marla trying to hit bottom? Why should she hit bottom? What purpose would that serve? Because the political explanation given for the narrator's self-contempt is not available in the case of Marla, and because we are given no explicit alternative explanation, we are led to believe that her self-hatred is idiosyncratic and inexplicable. She's just some crazy girl.[20]

Moreover if the political explanation in terms of emasculation does not account for Marla's lack of self-respect, then the political solution of reinstitutionalizing masculinity will not enable her recovery. How, then, can Marla be redeemed? Again, the narrative's ending supplies an answer. Marla must commit herself to the (now rehabilitated) narrator so together they can serve as the Adam and Eve of the new society. Marla, *qua* feminine, must be excluded from the revolt against femininity, but is, *qua* heterosexual female, instrumental to the success of a resurrected masculinist society. Alongside the narrator, she has found her "place"— the proper site of her redemption.

Marla, Bob and essentialism about gender

At the first support group meeting he attends (for men with testicular cancer), the narrator meets Bob, who turns out to be a pivotal character in the film. Bob has had his testicles removed and has developed breasts ("bitch tits") that are, in the narrator's words, "as big as gods are big."

It is in the arms of Bob, with his face nestled against Bob's enormous breasts, that the narrator first experiences the acceptance, comfort and emotional release that allow him finally to sleep. Later in the film, the narrator encounters Bob on the street. He greets him with genuine affection and learns in the course of their brief conversation, that Bob, too, has abandoned support groups in favor of fight club. When Tyler initiates Project Mayhem, Bob is one of his first recruits.

Tyler and the narrator's acceptance of Bob may seem in tension with my interpretation of *Fight Club*, which stresses the rejection of the feminine. First, it seems as though, through his relationship with Bob, the narrator *embraces*, rather than *rejects* the feminine—or, at any rate, he embraces (indeed literally) the *maternal* feminine. Second, Bob is permitted to join fight club and Project Mayhem. Does not Bob's inclusion undermine my claim that the revolution must exclude women since its aim is to counter the forces of feminization? And does not Bob's inclusion, therefore, undermine my claim that the film sees women's self-respect as appropriately achieved through association with a man, and not through revolution?

Given Tyler's (and derivatively, the narrator's) commitment to gender essentialism and to a strict nature/culture dichotomy, Bob's role in the film, I maintain, supports, rather than challenges, the interpretation I have given. By "gender essentialism" I mean the view that one's gender is part of or is determined by one's biological sex. Males, on this view, are, "by nature," masculine; women are, "by nature," feminine. The (purported) feminization of men perpetrated by consumer capitalism, is, on such an essentialist view, an attempt to make men into something they are not; it is an assault on their natures. It is in this respect (according to Tyler, anyway) misguided, if not immoral. And, it should be countered by strategies that will allow men to recover their masculinity.

This picture of gender is evinced primarily through expressions of Tyler's philosophy. Consider first, the fight club policy that requires members to strip down to nothing but their pants when they fight. This policy probably symbolizes a number of things,[21] but surely it symbolizes, in part, the shedding of the influence of culture on the biological male. Insofar as acculturation is a feminizing force, it also symbolizes the shedding of the feminine. When the external trappings of culture are discarded, what can be uncovered (through self-destruction) is the genuine or authentic man.

Consider second, Tyler's utopic vision of a world where men hunt, wearing durable leather clothes, while women pound corn and dry venison. While this vision harkens back to an earlier (perhaps mythical) time before modernity; it also endorses the normative primacy of the "natural" over the cultural. It is a vision where the presence and influence of culture is minimal and therefore people act in accordance with their "true" natures.

So, though the narrator may have found solace initially by embracing, in Bob, the maternal feminine, it is significant that Bob is biologically male. If the maternal feminine is the real source of healing for the contemporary man, why does the narrator find comfort in the arms of a feminized *male*? And why does Tyler tell the narrator that one of their problems is that they are part of "a generation of men raised by women"? Rather than seeing Bob as woman, I contend, we should see Bob as a male whose subjection to feminization has had the most acute manifestation. Bob has been transformed not merely psychologically, but physically. The narrator's initial relief comes to him in the form of affirmation from a fellow victim, who can serve also as a male mother figure.

Not only does the narrator find a male mother figure, he finds, in Tyler, a male intimate partner. Tyler is, for all intents and purposes, the narrator's lover, but, since they do not actually have sex, their relationship avoids the taint of femininity culturally associated with male homosexuality. In all respects except the sexual, Tyler and the narrator are intimate. They set up a household together. (The narrator compares them, in a scene depicting him straightening Tyler's tie, to Ozzie and Harriet.) They are emotionally committed to one another. Indeed, the narrator is consumed with jealously when Tyler begins a sexual relationship with Marla. And, by insisting that the narrator never talk to Marla about him or about what goes on in their house, Tyler isolates his sexual relationship with Marla from his, obviously more valued, relationship with the narrator.

So, the narrator has managed to find male substitutes to fill the roles in his life that would conventionally be filled by women. We can see this as an attempt to insulate himself from any genuinely feminine influence. It follows that Bob's inclusion in fight club and in Project Mayhem does *not* undermine my claim that eschewing the feminine is paramount to Tyler and the narrator's social program. In fact, it supports my view if we look at Bob, as I suggest Tyler would, as a feminized (and therefore damaged) male rather than as a personification of womanhood. We should see Bob as the literal embodiment of male victimization at the hands of an emasculating culture. On this view, to exclude Bob would be to exclude the man who perhaps most deserves to participate in the revolt against the forces of emasculation.

Summary

I have argued that *Fight Club's* narrative contains a revealing incoherence. It portrays both Marla and the narrator as burdened by self-contempt and driven to self-destruction. However, it implies that only the narrator is entitled to deliverance through the grueling therapy of personal trans-formation provided by fight club and by the protocol of social transformation undertaken through Project Mayhem. Hence it implies that either Marla is not entitled to redemption or that, if she is, she must find some alternative means. By positioning Marla, at the end, hand in hand with the narrator, who has been himself rehabilitated through the ordeal of fight club and Project Mayhem, the film suggests a fitting alternative means of redemption for Marla. In order for *her* to regain self-respect, she must join forces with a man. More specifically, she must attach herself to a man who has proven himself worthy of her love and support through his world-making activities. In relationship with such a man, Marla has finally acquired the "proper" grounds for self-worth and can begin the project of reclaiming her self-respect.

Notes

* I am grateful to Eric Hutton, Elijah Millgram, Keisha Ray, Kathryn Stockton and Thomas Wartenberg for their helpful feedback on this paper. I am also indebted to the undergraduates in my Philosophy and Film class taught in the Spring of 2010 for their inspiring and insightful discussions of *Fight Club*.

1 For example, Kant 1964 and Rawls 1971 may be interpreted in this way. See also, Williams 1973.

2 For example, Dillon 1992, 1997, and 2001, Hill 1991a and 1991b, Massey 1995, Middleton 2006, Sachs 1981, Telfer 1995 and Thomas 1978a and 1995.

3 See also, Darwall 1995 and Hudson 1980.

4 And other social hierarchies such as race, class and sexual orientation. For discussions of the connection between self-respect and oppression of

various sorts, see Bartky 1990a and 1990b, Boxill 1976 and 1984, Doppelt 1981, Held 1973, Hill 1991a, Mohr 1992, Thomas 1978b and Moody-Adams 1995.

5 By "people" here I refer primarily to my students. For a philosophical rejoinder to Hill's assessment of the Deferential Wife see Friedman 1985. For a response to Friedman see Baron 1985.

6 One reason my students give for thinking that the Deferential Wife does not lack self-respect is that she is proud to serve her husband. This reason is founded upon a confusion between recognition and evaluative self-respect. Another reason my students give is that to claim that the Deferential Wife is servile is to engage in victim blaming. This reason overlooks Hill's assertion that the issue of praise and blame is distinct from the issue of the presence or absence of the character flaw. Yet another reason my students give is that to the extent that the Deferential Wife herself *believes* that her attitude toward herself is appropriate, it is appropriate. This reason has to do with the issue of whether or not self-respect is an objective or subjective notion. See Massey 1995.

7 See also Antony 1988, De Beauvoir 1989, Holmstrom 1982, Mill 1989 and Wollstonecraft 2001.

8 We would likewise expect that men would stake their self-respect on their status as men.

9 The scare quotes indicate that if one's sense of worth is based upon her meeting the standards of femininity, rather than the standards of personhood, then she does not really have recognition self-respect.

10 See, for example, Turan 1999 and Nechak 1999.

11 See, for example, Dussere 2006. See also, Smith 1999 and Wilson 2006.

12 See Thompson 2004.

13 Ansen connects this scene with the film's (not fully acknowledged) homoerotic themes. He says, "All these guys masochistically lining up to be beaten up by Brad Pitt . . . The homoeroticism is off the charts, but *Fight Club* can't bring itself to account for it." See also, Denby 1999 and Lau unpublished.

14 Norton says in an interview that the film does not stress the significance of *committing* violence but rather of *being subject to it*. See McLean 1999.

15 Or perhaps perpetuating worse crimes. For a discussion of the fascistic elements of the film, see Hewitt 2006.

16 This is perhaps too general. It may be a predicament facing only white men. The absence of men of color in the film has been noted. See Lau unpublished, Locke unpublished and O'Hehir 1999. See also Stockton 2006.

17 The testicular cancer support group was called "Remaining Men Together."

18 This will no doubt go a long way in precluding the development of fashion, which will go a long way in precluding the development of a consumption-oriented society.

19 No doubt, women.

20 After the narrator meets (and sleeps with) Marla, he says to the narrator, "Man, you have got some *fucked up* friends!"
21 At one point, Tyler tells a new fight club member who is eager to fight, to "lose the tie." This suggests that stripping down has a leveling effect—it removes outward signs of social hierarchy among men.

Works cited

Ansen, David. 1999. "A Fistful of Darkness." *Newsweek*, Oct. 18: 77.

Antony, Louise M. 1988. "'Human Nature' and Its Role in Feminist Theory." In *Philosophy in a Feminist Voice*, ed., Janet Kourany. Princeton, NJ: Princeton University Press, pp. 61–91.

Aristotle. 1982. *The Politics*. Trans. T.A. Sinclair. New York: Penguin Books.

Baron, Marcia. 1985. "Servility, Critical Deference and the Deferential Wife." *Philosophical Studies* 48: 393–400.

Bartky, Sandra Lee. 1990a. "On Psychological Oppression." In *Femininity and Domination: Studies in the Phenomenology of Oppression*. London: Routledge, pp. 22–32.

Bartky, Sandra Lee. 1990b. "Shame and Gender." In *Femininity and Domination: Studies in the Phenomenology of Oppression*. London: Routledge, pp. 83–98.

Boxill, Bernard. 1976. "Self-Respect and Protest." *Philosophy and Public Affairs* 6: 58–69.

Boxill, Bernard. 1984. *Blacks and Social Justice*. Totowa, NJ: Rowman and Allenheld.

Darwall, Stephen. 1995. "Two Kinds of Respect." In *Dignity, Character and Self-Respect*, ed., Robin Dillon. New York: Routledge, pp. 181–197.

De Beauvoir, Simone. 1989. *The Second Sex*. Trans. H.M. Parshley. New York: Alfred A. Knopf.

Denby, David. 1999. "Boys Will Be Boys." *The New Yorker* 75, Oct. 18/25: 52–54.

Dillon, Robin. 1992. "How to Lose Your Self-Respect." *American Philosophical Quarterly* 29: 125–139.

Dillon, Robin. 1997. "Self-Respect: Moral, Emotional, Political." *Ethics* 107: 226–249.

Dillon, Robin. 2001. "Self-Forgiveness and Self-Respect." *Ethics* 112: 53–83.

Doppelt, Gerald. 1981. "Rawls' System of Justice: A Critique From the Left." *Nous* 15: 259–307.

Dussere, Erik. 2006. "Out of the Past, into the Supermarket: Consuming Film Noir." *Film Quarterly* 16: 16–27.

Freud, Sigmund. 1964. "Femininity." In *Standard Edition of the Complete Psychological Works*, Vol. 22. London: Hogarth Press.

Friedman, Marilyn. 1985. "Moral Integrity and the Deferential Wife." *Philosophical Studies* 47: 141–150.

Hewitt, Andrew. 2006. "Masochism and Terror: *Fight Club* and the Violence of Neo-Fascist Ressentiment." *Telos: A Quarterly Journal of Critical Thought* 136: 104–131.

Hill, Thomas, E., Jr. 1991a. "Servility and Self-Respect." In *Autonomy and Self-Respect*. Cambridge: Cambridge University Press, pp. 4–18.

Hill, Thomas, E., Jr. 1991b. "Self-Respect Reconsidered." In *Autonomy and Self-Respect*. Cambridge: Cambridge University Press, pp. 19–24.

Holmstrom, Nancy. 1982. "Do Women Have a Distinct Nature?" *The Philosophical Forum* 14: 25–42.

Hudson, Stephen D. 1980. "The Nature of Respect." *Social Theory and Practice* 6: 69–90.

Kant, Immanuel. 1960. *Observations on the Feeling of the Beautiful and the Sublime*. Trans. John T. Goldthwait. Berkeley: University of California Press.

Kant, Immanuel. 1964. *Groundwork of the Metaphysic of Morals*. Trans. H.J. Paton. New York: Harper and Row Publishers.

Kant, Immanuel. 1996. *The Metaphysics of Morals*. Trans. Mary Gregor. Cambridge: Cambridge University Press.

Lau, Kimberly. Unpublished. "Tricks of the Trade: Men At Work."

Locke, Brian. Unpublished. "The Cock of the Walk: Race and the Consolidation of White Masculinity in *Fight Club*."

Massey, Stephen J. 1995. "Is Self-Respect a Moral or a Psychological Concept?" In *Dignity, Character and Self-Respect*, ed., Robin Dillon. New York: Routledge, pp. 198–217.

McLean, Craig. 1999. "Public Enemy Number One: Edward Norton." *The Face*, Dec. www.edward-norton.org/articles/faceint.html (accessed 11 May 2011).

Middleton, David. 2006. "Three Types of Self-Respect." *Res Publica* 12: 59–76.

Mill, J.S. 1989. *The Subjection of Women*. Cambridge, MA: The M.I.T. Press.

Mohr, Richard. 1992. *Gay Ideas: Outing and Other Controversies*. Boston: Beacon Press.

Moody-Adams, Michelle. 1995. "Race, Class and the Social Construction of Self-Respect." In *Dignity, Character and Self-Respect*, ed., Robin Dillon. New York: Routledge, pp. 271–289.

Nechak, Paula. 1999. "Fight Club Dissects the Primal Nature of Men." *Seattle Post-Intelligencer*, Oct. 15. www.seattlepi.com/movies/fite15.shtml (accessed 11 May 2011).

O'Hehir, Andrew. 1999. "*Fight Club*." *Salon*, Oct. 15. http://salon.com/ent/movies/review/1999/10/15/fight_club/index.html (accessed 11 May 2011).

Rawls, John. 1971. *A Theory of Justice*. Cambridge, MA: Harvard University Press.

Rousseau, Jean-Jacques. 1979. *Emile*. Trans. Allan Bloom. New York: Basic Books.

Sachs, David. 1981. "How to Distinguish Self-Respect from Self-Esteem." *Philosophy and Public Affairs* 10: 346–360.

Smith, Gavin. 1999. "Inside Out: Gavin Smith goes one-on-one with David Fincher." *Film Comment*, Sept./Oct. www.filmlinc.com/fcm/9-10-99/fightclub.htm (accessed 11 May 2011).

Stockton, Kathryn Bond. 2006. *Beautiful Bottom, Beautiful Shame: Where Black Meets Queer*. Durham, NC: Duke University Press.

Telfer, Elizabeth. 1995. "Self-Respect." In *Dignity, Character and Self-Respect*, ed., Robin Dillon. New York: Routledge, pp. 107–116.

Thomas, Lawrence. 1978a. "Morality and Our Self-Concept." *Journal of Value Inquiry* 12: 258–268.

Thomas, Lawrence. 1978b. "Rawlsian Self-Respect and the Black Consciousness Movement." *The Philosophical Forum* 9: 303–314.

Thomas, Laurence. 1995. "Self-Respect: Theory and Practice." In *Dignity, Character and Self-Respect*, ed., Robin Dillon. New York: Routledge, pp. 251–270.

Thompson, Stacy. 2004. "Punk Cinema." *Cinema Journal* 43: 47–66.

Tuana, Nancy. 1993. *The Less Noble Sex: Scientific, Religious, and Philosophical Conceptions of Woman's Nature*. Indianapolis: Indiana University Press.

Turan, Kenneth. 1999. "*Fight Club*" *Los Angeles Times*, Oct. 15: 1.

Williams, Bernard. 1973. "The Idea of Equality." In *Problems of the Self*. Cambridge: Cambridge University Press, pp. 230–245.

Wilson, George. 2006. "Transparency and Twist in Narrative Fiction Film." *Thinking Through Cinema: Film as Philosophy*, eds., Murray Smith and Thomas Wartenberg. Oxford: Blackwell Publishing, pp. 81–96.

Wollstonecraft, Mary. 2001. *A Vindication of the Rights of Woman*. New York: Modern Library.

Suggested further readings

Baron, Marcia. 1985. "Servility, Critical Deference and the Deferential Wife." *Philosophical Studies* 48: 393–400.

Bauer, Nancy. 2005. "Cogito Ergo Film: Plato, Decartes and *Fight Club*." In *Film as Philosophy: Essays on Cinema After Wittgenstein and Cavell*, eds., Rupert Read and Jerry Goodenough. New York: Palgrave MacMillan, pp. 39–56.

Boxill, Bernard. 1976. "Self-Respect and Protest." *Philosophy and Public Affairs* 6: 58–69.

Dillon, Robin. 1992. "How to Lose Your Self-Respect." *American Philosophical Quarterly* 29: 125–139.

Dillon, Robin, ed. 1995. *Dignity, Character and Self-Respect*. New York: Routledge.

Dillon, Robin. 1997. "Self-Respect: Moral, Emotional, Political." *Ethics* 107: 226–249.

Dillon, Robin. 2001. "Self-Forgiveness and Self-Respect." *Ethics* 112: 53–83.

Dillon, Robin. 2004a. "Kant on Arrogance and Self-Respect." In *Setting the Moral Compass*, ed. Cheshire Calhoun. New York: Oxford University Press, pp. 191–216.

Dillon, Robin. 2004b. "'What's a Woman Worth? What's Life Worth? Without Self-Respect!': On the Value of Evaluative Self-Respect." In *Moral Psychology*, eds., Peggy DesAutels and Margaret Walker. Oxford: Rowman and Littlefield, pp. 47–66.

Dussere, Erik. 2006. "Out of the Past, into the Supermarket: Consuming Film Noir." *Film Quarterly* 16: 16–27.

Friedman, Marilyn. 1985. "Moral Integrity and the Deferential Wife." *Philosophical Studies* 47: 141–150.

Hewitt, Andrew. 2006. "Masochism and Terror: *Fight Club* and the Violence of Neo-Fascist Ressentiment." *Telos: A Quarterly Journal of Critical Thought* 136: 104–131.

Hill, Thomas, E., Jr. 1991a. "Servility and Self-Respect." In *Autonomy and Self-Respect*. Cambridge: Cambridge University Press, pp. 4–18.

Hill, Thomas, E., Jr. 1991b. "Self-Respect Reconsidered." In *Autonomy and Self-Respect*. Cambridge: Cambridge University Press, pp. 19–24.

Kant, Immanuel. 1964. *Groundwork of the Metaphysic of Morals*. Trans. H.J. Paton. New York: Harper and Row Publishers.

Kant, Immanuel. 1996. *The Metaphysics of Morals*. Trans. Mary Gregor. Cambridge: Cambridge University Press.

Massey, Stephen J. 1983. "Kant on Self-Respect." *Journal of the History of Philosophy* 21: 57–73.

Meyers, Diana T. 1986. "The Politics of Self-Respect: A Feminist Perspective." *Hypatia* 1: 83–100.

Middleton, David. 2006. "Three Types of Self-Respect." *Res Publica* 12: 59–76.

Postow. B.C. 1978–79. "Economic Dependence and Self-Respect." *The Philosophical Forum* 10: 181–205.

Stark, Cynthia. 1997. "The Rationality of Valuing Oneself: A Critique of Kant on Self-Respect." *Journal of the History of Philosophy* 34: 65–82.

Superson, Anita. 2010. "The Deferential Wife Revisited: Agency and Moral Responsibility." *Hypatia* 25: 253–275.

Thompson, Stacy. 2004. "Punk Cinema." *Cinema Journal* 43: 47–66.

Wilson, George. 2006. "Transparency and Twist in Narrative Fiction Film." *Thinking Through Cinema: Film as Philosophy*, eds., Murray Smith and Thomas Wartenberg. Oxford: Blackwell Publishing, pp. 81–96.

Chapter 5

George M. Wilson and Sam Shpall

UNRAVELING THE TWISTS OF *FIGHT CLUB*[1]

D AVID FINCHER'S FIGHT CLUB (1999) is surely one of the most striking "twist" movies of the recent period in American films – a period that seems to have reveled in "twisted" audiovisual narration. The movie is famous for revealing that it has implicitly featured a mode of visual narration that is surprisingly "subjective" in an unusual way. By suppressing the revelation of narrational subjectivity until the end, the movie becomes an instance of unreliable audiovisual narration in movies, although the precise character of the unreliability in this case deserves to be explored. In the first part of this paper, we attempt to give a reasonably precise specification of the chief kinds of "subjective presentation" that are at work in much of this film. More narrowly, we review some of the main ways that a shot or sequence in a movie may be thought of as "subjective," and we argue that *Fight Club* exploits a fairly common mode of "subjective inflection" in the telling but does so in a strikingly sophisticated way. In the second part of the paper, we turn to thematic issues, and we argue that, although the movie foregrounds a certain critique of the ills of contemporary culture, this foregrounding is significantly misleading. Indeed, we believe that many commentators *have been* misled, and we offer an alternative account of the perspective on Tyler Durden (Brad Pitt) and his view of things that the movie more plausibly depicts.

Part I

Introduction

One of the characteristic marks of classical narrative films is that their audio/visual narration is, in a certain sense, transparent. Very roughly, this means that: (1) most of the shots in these movies are understood as providing the audience with "objective" or intersubjectively accessible views of the fictional characters, actions, and situations depicted in the film; and that (2) where the shots or sequences are not to be construed as objective, there is a reasonably clear marking of the fact that they are, in one of several different ways, "subjective." Of course, "subjective shots and sequences" come in various modes. For instance, some shots and sequences depict the perceptual field of a particular character. Others depict a character's visual imaginings, memories, dreams, or hallucinations. Still others render in visual terms the content of something that some character is verbally reporting or describing. This short list of possibilities is obviously not exhaustive, and the individual "subjective" modes deserve lengthier discussion. Nevertheless, let us say that (1) and (2) give us, as a crude first approximation, a specification of the norm of the *transparency of narration* in classical narrative film. Although the conception that these conditions jointly express has a recognizable intuitive import, it is not easy to elaborate the conception more sharply. The concept of an objective shot or sequence in fiction films is problematic and, correlatively, so are the various concepts of subjective depiction. Moreover, the nature and functioning of the factors that contextually mark the epistemic status of a movie segment (that is, a shot or edited sequence) can be surprisingly elusive.

The "twist" films we are thinking of come in several distinguishable kinds. Here we will be chiefly concerned with movies in which the cinematic narration, as the audience eventually comes to realize, represents the narrative action in terms of the subjective perspective of a particular character, although, in general, that action has not been represented from the perceptual point of view of the character in question. That is, the narration stands outside the "focalizing" character, regularly presenting him or her within the frame. Still, at the same time, the narration reflects the problematic or idiosyncratic way in which the character sees or imagines the relevant fictional history to have transpired. In a sense to be explained later, these films involve image tracks that have notably been "subjectively inflected from an impersonal vantage point." Moreover, this narrational strategy is not clearly marked until very late in the movie.[2] Our chief example of this phenomenon is Fight Club, in which a particularly global application of this kind of subjective inflection is achieved.

We will proceed in the following fashion. First, we will distinguish between several different kinds of subjective shots and sequence. It is important to do this because these different modes are easily run together. Some of the modes that we will be identifying are quite familiar, but others, for example, the impersonal, subjective inflection of Fight Club, are not. Second, we will discuss the fact that a film or a segment of film may be systematically subjective in one or another mode, although this fact about the narration is not made clear in the movie until after or just before the segment or feature is winding up. This device of setting up an epistemic ambiguity in the film narration that fails to be signaled in the relevant context sets up the possibility of a kind of systematic unreliability in the presentation of the story. This is a chief aspect of the narration of Fight Club, but it is crucial to be fairly specific about how the unreliability comes to be established. We will, along the way, describe some cases of epistemic unreliability in movies that contrast with the special deviousness of the Fincher film. Finally, we discuss at some length an interpretation of Fight Club that helps make sense of the twists and turns that figure in its narrative.

Point-of-view shots: subjectively inflected, subjectively uninflected and subjectively saturated

We will begin by introducing some reflections on the concept of a "subjective" shot and about some of the important subdivisions within the category. These considerations will be pretty rough and ready, since each category to be discussed involves considerable variation and complexity, but we will say enough to argue for two points. First, subjective segments of the sorts that we will examine involve at least two different notions of "the subjective." Second, we will show why it is crucial for us to have at least a schematic overview of a number of the main kinds of subjective shots.[3] Later, we will distinguish, from the more familiar kinds, one special type of subjective shot – what we will call "impersonal but subjectively inflected shots." This category does not seem to be adequately delineated in the literature, and we will highlight its interest later in the discussion. We will start out by considering segments whose "subjective" character is more or less clearly indicated in their immediate context. In the last section of the first part of the paper, we will turn to some issues that are raised by segments whose "subjective" status has not been marked immediately in this fashion – segments of nontransparent narration, in other words.

Among the shots commonly deemed to be "subjective," one naturally thinks first of veridical point-of-view (POV) shots. These are shots that represent (at least approximately) the visual perspective, anchored in an implicit visual vantage point, of a designated character at a given time. Although this is the simplest case, it is not really clear why veridical POV shots are regularly counted as "subjective." It is often said that viewers are meant to imagine that they are seeing the relevant fictional items and events "through the eyes" of the relevant character. In some sense, this is no doubt true, but the sense in question is not so easy to pin down. In our opinion, what film viewers imagine seeing in a veridical POV shot are the fictional circumstances that the character perceives, and viewers imagine that they are seeing the depicted fictional material from a visual perspective that coincides more or less with the visual perspective of the observing character in the film. Nevertheless, certain tempting mis-conceptions need to be avoided. As Kendall Walton and one of the present authors (Wilson) have each argued elsewhere, film viewers, in so imagining, do not imagine either that they are, at that moment, identical with the movie character or even that they occupy the implied vantage point of the character within the movie's fictional space.[4] Rather, it is to be imagined that the visual perspective offered on the screen arises from the same vantage point as the vantage point that fictionally the character is occupying at the time of his or her viewing.

So in what sense is a veridical POV shot subjective? After all, if what viewers imagine seeing in the shot is, in the first instance, the objective circumstances in the fictional world that fall within the character's gaze, then the depicted content of the shot is not subjective. Both the film viewers and the viewing character are being supplied with intersubjective information about these observable circumstances. In this respect at least, the information that is fictionally presented in the shot is just as "objective" as the information in shots whose visual perspective is not identified with that of any character. Of course, the veridical POV shot simultaneously makes it fictional that the character is seeing the circumstances before his or her eyes and seeing them from the vantage point implicit in the shot. And yet, a non-POV shot that showed the same character gazing at the same fictional circumstances (for example, in an over-the-shoulder shot of those circumstances) would generate more or less the same fictional truths about the character's seeing and what it is he or she sees. However, such a shot would not normally be deemed subjective. If we were to suppose that the visual contents of the POV shot are to be imagined as representing the private field of vision of the perceiving character, then that putative fact would yield an obvious sense in which POV shots are "subjective." Nevertheless, it is doubtful that this is a part of what viewers normally imagine or are meant to imagine when they watch veridical POV shots. Hence, it is correspondingly doubtful that this explanation of POV subjectivity should be endorsed. The subjectivity of veridical POV shots may well consist in nothing more than the coincidence of vantage point between the onscreen imagery and the character's visual perspective. Or, alternatively, it may be that POV shots are thought of as subjective because the occupation of their vantage points by a fictional perceiver always raises the question, at least potentially, of whether the shots in question are fictionally veridical. By contrast, given the strong but defeasible expectation of transparency, non-POV shots are tacitly and almost automatically construed as offering film viewers intersubjectively accessible information about the objective scene in view. We will leave this question about the general nature of the subjectivity of POV shots unresolved, but we want to stress the fact that the sense in which veridical POV shots are subjective is really pretty weak.

On the other hand, there are POV shots and sequences in which a viewer is expected to imagine something about the phenomenal qualities or contents of a character's field of vision. We are all familiar with POV shots that are, as we will say, subjectively inflected. That is, a range of the visual properties of the shot are supposed to represent subjective enhancements and distortions of the character's field of vision at the time. For instance, when the character is drunk, dizzy, or otherwise perceptually disoriented, then special effects of focus, lighting, filtering, or camera movement may be employed to depict the way these psychological conditions have affected the character's visual experience. Similarly, consider a POV shot in which a character is seeing items in his or her immediate environment, but the character's field of vision also includes some hallucinatory objects or events. For example, in a POV shot, some character may be represented as looking into his or her garage and hallucinating a pink aardvark on the car. Of course, partially hallucinated perceptual structure shots of this type occur in many films. Robert Altman's *Images* (1972), which is itself a kind of epistemological twist film, features many partially hallucinatory POV shots from the heroine's (Susannah York) perspective, and the psychological drama of the movie is centrally built up around them. In any case, we are stipulating that these partially hallucinated POV shots are to count as subjectively inflected as well. Since certain internal properties of a character's perceptual state are represented in such shots, they are understood to be "subjective" in a straightforward sense. Normally, the objective and subjective aspects of the image and the way the two are related are specified clearly enough in the immediate film context. Let us say that these aspects and the relations between them constitute "the epistemic structure" of the pertinent shot or sequence. That is, in standard segments of this type, it is plainly indicated by the context that the character is actually seeing a certain fictional situation before his or her eyes and that he or she is also seeing the situation from a certain visual perspective that is subjectively inflected in a certain way – the way that is depicted on the screen.

Correspondingly, film viewers imagine seeing the same fictional objects and events as the character, and they imagine seeing them from the very same inflected visual perspective. On one extreme of the subjectively inflected mode, the subjective inflection of the visual perspective may be total. That is, movie spectators are to imagine that the character's visual perspective is completely determined by his or her present state of dreaming, hallucination, or inner visualization of one sort or another and to imagine themselves seeing those private visual contents. We will call such shots "subjectively saturated." In this sort of case, spectators are mandated to refrain from imagining that they are being provided with information about whatever fictional environment lies outside the character's mind. So, is it correct to say that spectators imagine seeing anything in such cases of total subjective saturation? Well, should we say that people who are subject to total hallucinations are seeing something? In one sense yes, and in another sense, perhaps, no. No because they are blinded to their environment by their total hallucination. Yes because they "see" the things that they hallucinate. In the case of film spectatorship, if the viewed segment is contextually marked to indicate that it depicts, for example, what a character is dreaming, then spectators do imagine seeing something, but it is "seeing" in the more inclusive sense. What they imagine "seeing" is what they recognize to be the visual contents of the character's dream.

However, none of this implies that the film viewers imagine themselves dreaming that very dream. More generally, it seems to us that visually subjective shots (whether the shots are subjectively inflected or saturated) never call on spectators to imagine that they are identical with the visualizing character nor that they are actually having the fictional visualizer's visual experiences. Film spectators merely imagine that the visual perspective presented onscreen coincides in its important, salient respects with the phenomenal qualities and contents of the character's visual experience, but not that those subjective visual experiences are their own. (This generalizes a point we mentioned earlier.)

And yet, is the imagined seeing by one person of the private visual experiences of another really coherent? It depends, we believe, on how deep we expect the coherence of what viewers imagine in such a case to be. The following is one way we might imagine seeing the visual contents of someone else's dream. We can imagine that neuroscientists have discovered in exhaustive detail the physical basis of dreaming. Implementing their discoveries in video technology, they come to have the capacity to introduce sensitive probes into a dreamer's brain and record the dream-relevant electrochemical activity that is taking place. Suitably transforming that recorded information, they are able to project a phenomenologically accurate visual representation of the dreamer's dream imagery on a large monitor above the dreamer's head. Thus, anyone suitably placed before the monitor is able to see the contents and phenomenal qualities of the projected dream.[5] If we can imagine this scenario, then we can imagine seeing (as observers) the contents of someone else's dream, and we can imagine this without imagining that we are having the dream experiences ourselves. In a similar way, when viewers watch a dream sequence in film, they imagine themselves seeing the contents of the fictional dream, but they do not imagine themselves to be experiencing that very dream. We are claiming that we can imagine dreams to have a kind of public visual accessibility, but we don't claim that what we imagine is philosophically or scientifically coherent in any substantial detail. Almost surely it is not. (The superficial coherence may well depend on our tendency to imagine our dreams as if they were movies in our heads.) After all, a fair amount of what we imagine to ourselves is only superficially coherent in just this way. Also, we are not supposing that when we imagine seeing someone's dream in the movies we imagine this by imagining that some agency of dream engineering has projected the dreamer's experience on the movie screen in front of us. On the contrary, we simply do not imagine much of anything in particular about how the dreamer's visual perspective has been presented to our view. It is imaginatively indeterminate how this has come to be, but this indeterminacy is nothing special. In the same way, we imagine almost nothing about the means or mechanisms by which the movie's impersonal views of objective circumstances in the story have come to be fictionally visible to us.

Impersonal shots that are subjectively inflected

Let us now consider an important way in which the epistemic structure of a segment may be even more complicated. All the types of subjective shot that we have described are to be contrasted with another kind of subjective shot. It is a type that is not as frequently deployed as, say, POV shots, but it is common enough in conventional narrative films. These are non-POV shots (more broadly, impersonal shots) that are subjectively inflected but do not share their vantage point with the visual perspective of any character in the film. Here is one simple and fairly well-known example. In *Murder My Sweet* (Edward Dmytryk, 1944), Phillip Marlowe (Dick Powell) has been knocked out and drugged. When he eventually comes to, we 'see' him stagger around the room. However, these shots of him are, in a certain respect, clearly subjective. In voice-over, Marlowe describes his clouded perceptual experience, and the shots with which we are presented look as though they had been filtered through smoke and spider webs. The look of the shots in this respect is obviously meant to correspond to key aspects of the way that things are looking to Marlowe in his drugged condition, but the screen image here does not purport to give us his actual visual perspective. As in an objective shot, we imagine seeing Marlowe as he wanders around the room, but, at the same time, we do not imagine that the room is filled with smoke and spider webs. The look of smoke and spider webs is imagined to represent certain phenomenal properties present in Marlowe's field of vision. In this example, we are prompted to the conclusion that these features of the image are subjective because Marlowe, in voice-over, tells us that this is what his drugged visual experience is like. So, we imagine seeing Marlowe and his actions from a visual perspective he does not and could not occupy. Moreover, it is a visual perspective that is not experienced by anyone else in the film. Still, we are keyed to suppose that the pertinent phenomenal properties included in the onscreen visual perspective reflect specific qualitative inflections with which we imagine the detective's visual perspective to be suffused. This constitutes a third kind of subjective shot, and we will call it "an impersonal, subjectively inflected shot." In this example, we imagine ourselves seeing Marlowe and his actions from an unoccupied visual perspective that is subjectively inflected in specific ways. The concept of "impersonal but subjectively inflected shots" should be understood strictly to entail that the phenomenal qualities or contents of a character's perceptual experience are mirrored in the shot.

These cases should be distinguished from still another type of psychologically charged impersonal shot. Mitry points out that there are impersonal shots that pick out objects and events that have been shown to be perceived by a character and present them in a way that illuminates the psychological significance they have for the character.[6] For instance, the clenched fist of one character, Jones, may be shot in a close-up that expresses the looming threat that Smith feels when he notices the clenching of Jones's hand. The hypothetical shot is a close-up, but Jones is standing at a considerable distance from Smith. The shot is therefore not literally a shot from Jones's visual perspective, although, in its narrative context, it may tell us a fair amount about Jones's reactive thoughts and emotions. This would be a good example of what Mitry refers to as a "semi-subjective shot." Nevertheless, since the shot does not show us anything about the phenomenal character of Jones's visual field, it is not a subjectively inflected impersonal shot, as we have introduced that concept. We have the impression that Mitry's category may include impersonal, subjectively inflected shots, although he never describes an instance of this narrower kind. The danger is that he effectively conflates them with other types of impersonal shots whose chief function is to imply something about a character's cognitive or affective states.

Still, one might worry that our characterization of subjectively inflected impersonal shots verges on inconsistency. The characterization seems to ask us to suppose that film viewers imagine that they are visually presented with a subjectively inflected field of vision, but a field of vision that impossibly belongs to no one. Of course, if we assumed that the various non-POV shots in a transparent film depict, in the first instance, the perceptual experience of an invisible camera-witness, then there would be no problem here. We could readily allow that subjectively inflected images present the phenomenal contents and qualities of the field of vision of this implicit witness. However, the general identification of the camera with such an invisible spectator is, for well-canvassed reasons, quite implausible. It is equally implausible to posit that such a witness pops into fictional existence only to accommodate the subjectivity of these impersonal shots. As one of the present authors (Wilson) has argued before, there really is no incoherence in the concept. The visual perspective of a shot is not to be identified with the field of vision of a character, explicit or implicit in the fiction, unless the film narration specifically establishes such an identity. We imagine the shots in Murder My Sweet as showing us Marlowe's action from the visual perspective a person would have if he or she were viewing the action from a certain vantage point and if he or she were afflicted with the type of clouded vision that Marlowe is experiencing. This visual perspective is not fictionally identical with anyone's actual field of vision.

The distinction between veridical POV shots and impersonal subjectively inflected shots underscores the treacherous ambiguity of the phrase "point of view," even when that phrase is constrained to apply to matters of strict visual experience. Shots of the latter kind show us the character's perceptual point of view in one sense (they delineate the qualitative nature of his or her perception) but not in the other (they do not present the vantage point from which he or she looks). Impersonal subjectively inflected shots and sequences range from the trivial to the rich and intricate. A segment in which a character is shown pondering some decision while the character's visualized thoughts appear as if they were projected behind him or her is subjectively inflected in a trivial way. However, subjectively inflected shots can exhibit a nuanced epistemic structure. They offer the possibility of directly showing the audience intersubjectively accessible information about a character and his or her behavior while, at the same time, presenting important facets of the character's private perceptual impressions. We can see the character and, to a significant degree, see with him or her at the same time. Such shots have the further potential of insinuating some outside comment from the filmmaker about the relations between the characters' depicted states of sentience and the actions they produce.

We can invoke a larger sense of the more interesting possibilities here if we remind ourselves of the famous shot from Hitchcock's *Vertigo* (1958) in which Scottie (James Stewart) kisses and embraces Judy (Kim Novak) just after she has remade herself as Madeline.[7] The couple is in Judy's hotel room and, as they kiss, the camera (or so it seems) begins to track around them. In the course of the shot, the hotel setting gradually fades into blackness and is replaced by a slightly dimmed view of the stable in San Juan Bautista – the place where Scottie had kissed Madeline just before her apparent death. Still embracing Judy, he looks around him, appearing troubled and disoriented. The background view of the stable fades back to black, and the hotel room gradually reappears, bathed now in a ghostly green. This shot contains additional complications that we will ignore, but the effects of the features we have already mentioned are tricky to characterize accurately.

We take it that this is a subjectively inflected shot, but the inflection is more elaborate than in the shot from *Murder My Sweet*. Presumably, the circling "camera" vantage point is meant to depict the nature of the overwhelming emotion Scottie feels at that moment, and it is an emotion that is here being linked to the film's recurrent motif of vertigo. The background shot of the stable represents a hallucinated memory image – an image that has flooded into Scottie's consciousness, superimposing itself on his view of the hotel room. Presumably, the experience is so unexpected and so vivid that it causes the bewilderment that is registered in Scotty's face. So, what is it that film viewers imagine seeing in this extended shot? They imagine seeing Scotty's and Judy's intense embrace in the Empire Hotel, and they imagine seeing the embrace from an impersonal moving vantage point that circles around the couple. Spectators also imagine that the circling visual perspective expresses the vertiginous sensations that Scotty is experiencing at the time. When the view of the stable appears, they imagine seeing Scotty hallucinating as he holds Judy/Madeline to him and the content of what he is then hallucinating. What is more, the dynamics of this non-POV shot suggest a narrational comment on the narrative situation. For example, they hint at the entrapment of both characters in their private obsessions and the uncanny nature of the circumstances that these obsessions have led them to create. We say that this subjectively inflected shot is impersonal, but this application of the term should not mislead. The vantage point is impersonal – it is not occupied by anyone in the fiction – but what the shot expresses about the characters is not emotionally impersonal. It is engaged and sympathetic, expressing the filmmaker's attitudes toward the scene.

Unmarked subjective inflections

In the example from *Vertigo*, the structure of objective and subjective elements of the shot is elaborate, but its structure and import are reasonably clear. Viewers may differ about interpretative details, but it is apparent that we are seeing Judy and Scottie embrace in the hotel room as Scottie flashes back in memory to the earlier incident in the stable. The epistemic structures of the segments in our earlier examples are simpler and, correspondingly, the structures are even more plainly delineated in their immediate narrative contexts. So, these are shots and sequences in which the norm of narrational transparency has been locally preserved. However, there are numerous exceptions to the practice of immediate transparency. Even in classical narrative films, there are many cases in which the epistemic structure of a segment is not specified straight away when the segment occurs. In fact, there are many instances in which there is some deliberate delay in identifying a significant aspect of the segment's epistemic structure. Indeed, in a number of these examples, the specification of structure is long postponed, sometimes for almost the whole length of the film. In these instances, the nature of the epistemic structure of particular earlier segments is eventually settled at narrative closure.

Epistemological twist films are defined by the fact that global aspects of the epistemic structure of their narration are clarified, in a surprising way, only toward the end of the movie. Hitchcock's *Stage Fright* (1950) opens with a notorious "lying" flashback. One character (Richard Todd) verbally tells another (Jane Wyman) about what happened when a murder took place and, as he narrates his story, there is a long visual sequence that seems to be a flashback to the events that he is recounting. It is only at the film's conclusion that we learn that this character has been lying and that the relevant sequence has to be reconstrued as merely a visual illustration of the content of the liar's false assertions. Of course, this segment is "subjective" in still a different sense – it is the rendering of what a character has verbally reported. In this instance, the report is false and, for present purposes, what is important is that the movie suppresses the fact that it is false until the story's end approaches.

In Fritz Lang's *The Woman in the Window* (1944), we discover near the conclusion that the whole story of Professor Wanley's (Edward G. Robinson) involvement with a treacherous *femme fatale* (Joan Bennett) – an involvement that leads him to murder her lover – has been a nightmare that the professor has been dreaming. Almost nothing in the style of the film's visual narration prompts us to suppose that what we are seeing is a dream. That disclosure is simply announced by showing Wanley as he finally wakes up in a chair in his club. In both these cases and others like them, the movies wind up revealing an epistemological twist, but the twist, as it is handled here, can seem arbitrary and artificial. Viewers often feel cheated by the tricks. Be this as it may, suppose that long-delayed and suppressed issues of epistemic structure are eventually settled in a given film. Should we say that the movie satisfies the norm of narrational transparency? Must epistemic structure be clear more or less continuously throughout the film? We do not think it matters much what stipulation we adopt, but the "twist" movies certainly violate at least the classical implementations of transparency.

Returning to *The Woman in the Window* for a moment, there is a question about what viewers, who already know about the dream twist, imagine seeing in the scenes that relate the contents of the dream. As one first watches the relevant segments, one imagines seeing, for example, the professor murder his romantic rival. However, after it has been revealed that Wanley has been dreaming all along, do viewers still imagine themselves as having seen the murder? Or, alternatively, when viewers see the movie a second time and know that Wanley dreams his adventures, then, as they rewatch the murder scene, do they still imagine seeing the professor commit the crime? Or, at this juncture, do they merely imagine seeing the contents of his dream? Our own strong inclination is to say the following. Both the first time and the second time that viewers watch the scene, they do imagine seeing Professor Wanley kill his rival. The murder is, as it were, visually present on the screen. However, on the first viewing, while implicitly accepting the assumption of transparency, viewers suppose that the murder actually takes place (in the overall world of the story). Seeing the same scene again, they have learned that this supposition about the status of what they have imagined seeing is false.

Thus, on a second viewing, they continue to imagine seeing Wanley perform the murder, but this time they imagine, that is, they suppose, that the murder is merely something that the professor fictionally has dreamed. Hence, we need to draw a distinction between what viewers imagine seeing in a stretch of film and the imaginative suppositions that they adopt about the epistemic and ontological standing of the things and events that they imagine seeing. The "core" contents of what viewers imagine seeing remains roughly the same from viewing to viewing. It is what the film viewers imagine (suppose) about the epistemological status of what they imagine seeing that alters so sharply. Compare this with a case in which there is a notable change of dramatic aspect for the viewer between two viewings of the same scene. Watching a close-up of Octave in *The Rules of the Game* (Jean Renoir, 1939), the viewer might, the first time through, imagine seeing Octave's (Jean Renoir) face as expressing one set of emotions, but imagine seeing, the next time around, a different mix of feeling and motivation in Octave's countenance. Here, we are inclined to say that there has been a change in the "core" content of what the viewer has imagined seeing from one showing to another. The very look of Octave's face, as the viewer imagines it each time, has changed. In our opinion, this contrasts with the situation of the viewer before and after the disclosure of a systematic epistemological twist.

Finally, let us explain this claim by focusing specifically on *Fight Club*. First, here is the barest skeleton of its plot. An unnamed character played by Edward Norton – we will call him "Jack"[8] – meets an intense, charismatic young soap salesman, Tyler Durden (Brad Pitt). Jack and Tyler form a close friendship, live together in a house on Paper Street, and become founders of a series of underground fight clubs – clubs in which marginalized young men meet together and pound each other into pulp in arranged fights. Jack has a tentative, sour friendship with a woman, Marla (Helena Bonham Carter), but it is Tyler and Marla who come to have an explosive sexual affair. The fight clubs evolve into Project Mayhem, a quasi-fascistic organization of urban guerrillas who aim to destroy the credit-based foundations of the contemporary economic system. Tyler is the moving force behind Project Mayhem, while Jack is apparently a more passive fellow traveler in that enterprise. What we discover, as the narrative concludes, is that Tyler is the hallucinated ideal projection of Jack's volatile and distorted psyche. Jack imagines seeing Tyler in his company and he imagines that they regularly talk and

Figure 5.1 Marla entering a self-help group

interact. Nevertheless, Tyler is a creation of Jack's imagination. We also find out, late in the movie, that Jack has sometimes adopted the Tyler persona and acted under that fantasized identity. For instance, he travels around the country promoting the fight clubs and expanding Project Mayhem. Apparently, Jack has no memory of what he does as Tyler, and it is only in the scene of revelation that we are directly shown a moment in which Jack assumes the role of Tyler.

However, we are repeatedly shown scenes in which Jack and Tyler appear together – conversing, fighting, engaging in horseplay, and so on. These are the scenes that most straightforwardly raise the question of the overall coherence of the film's narration. After all, Tyler really does not exist, so how do we construe his repeated appearances in the film's narration? Take, for example, all the scenes in which we imagine seeing Jack and Tyler together in their house on Paper Street. It simply does not make sense to suppose that nothing of what we imagine seeing in this setting actually took place. Many of the events portrayed in these inflected scenes have causal consequences that turn out to be real in the ultimate fiction of the film. The chemical burn that Tyler inflicts on the back of Jack's hand is just one rather emblematic illustration of the point. What we have to imagine, when we consider the film in retrospect, is that Jack does utter most of the things we hear him say and performs most of the actions that we observe. We are also meant to imagine that, on these occasions, Jack is simultaneously hallucinating Tyler's presence, his deeds, and speeches, and that Jack is responding to these fantasized occurrences. Characteristically, the two characters are presented together in the frame and shot from an impersonal vantage point. However, in light of the culminating disclosure, we are forced to look back and reconstrue these sequences as perspectivally impersonal but subjectively inflected. They are inflected to represent in a single shot both Jack's actual behavior and the content of his concurrent delirious experience.

That these segments are to be understood as inflected versions of an otherwise objective situation is implied by the following considerations: there are scenes in which Jack and Tyler are together in the kitchen, scenes that are either preceded or followed by Marla's entrance into that room. When she is there, Tyler is always absent. The scenes between Jack and Marla would seem to be patently objective, and the continuity of the space between these scenes and the adjacent sequences with Tyler indicates that Jack remains objectively present in the kitchen throughout. But when Tyler also seems to be present, Jack is actually by himself and talking to a hallucinated figure. Near the end of the movie, as the truth begins to dawn on Jack, we are given several short shots that show Jack acting by himself in situations where earlier we had seen Jack and Tyler acting together. These later shots model for us what we are now to imagine about the real circumstances after we have discounted for the subjective inflection. In certain scenes, the fantasized relationships are even more complicated. When Tyler finally explains the psychological state of affairs to Jack, he says: "Sometimes you're still you—sometimes you imagine yourself watching me." At this juncture, there is a shot of Jack lecturing the members of the fight club, echoing an earlier shot in which Tyler delivered the lecture. The late shot establishes that it was Jack who had spoken these words, imagining himself as Tyler. However, in the earlier counterpart scene, we were also given brief glimpses of Jack standing in the crowd and gazing at Tyler. So, presumably, Jack both hallucinates being Tyler and being himself (qua Jack) watching Tyler perform. In any case, given the ultimate perspective of the film, we are asked to re-imagine earlier critical scenes either in these kinds of terms or in minor variants thereof.

The sequences with Jack and Tyler constitute the most extensive and daring uses of impersonal subjective inflection with which we are familiar. They are particularly audacious because the massive subjective inflection is left unspecified until so late in the movie. The global narrational structure of the film is cleverly designed. Jack is the intermittent voice-over narrator of the film, and the film's narration is probably best understood as an audio/visual rendering of the narrative that he is verbally recounting. The film narration includes many segments (most of the ones in which Tyler does not appear) that are, even with hindsight, genuinely objective. However, as we will see in a moment, it also interpolates some shorter sequences that are marked in the immediate context as subjective depictions of Jack's fantasies. So the narration, in an apparently conventional manner, moves between depiction of the objective world of the fiction and the private perceptions and fantasies of the main character. The twist, of course, is the fact that the full extent of the inflection of the narration of Jack's consciousness has been systematically obscured.

The objective presentation of the story, then, is troubled from the outset by odd, seemingly unmotivated incursions from the contents of Jack's mind. At the beginning of the movie, we are given a POV shot from Jack's perspective as he looks out the window of an office building, but his view out the window morphs seamlessly into a dizzying traveling shot that careens down through the building and into the underground parking garage below. This highly dynamic subjective shot encapsulates in a flash Jack's memory of the bomb that Project Mayhem has planted in a van that is sitting in the garage. Also, on two occasions, we see Jack's surreal daydream of wandering through an icy cavern. The first time he is accompanied by a playful penguin, the second time he discovers Marla there. Or, taking a business flight, Jack wishes in voice-over for a plane crash and hallucinates the disaster in grim detail. This hallucination immediately precedes his meeting Tyler, who is sitting next to him in the airplane.

Figure 5.2 Tyler as the narrator realizes they are the same person

All these segments are subjectively saturated, but there are also short instances of subjective inflection, plainly identifiable as such. Thus Jack sits on the toilet, reading a house decoration catalogue, and the movie cuts to a tracking shot that explores his fantasy of his apartment fully furnished with IKEA-like products, each item shown on screen as if it were labeled by its caption in the catalogue. Subsequently, we see Jack, having risen from the toilet still in his underwear, amble through his apartment (with its subjectively captioned contents), and go to the refrigerator. Or prior to the point at which Tyler makes his entrance as a definite character in the film, various "objective" shots of sundry circumstances incorporate brief, usually subliminal, images of him. It is as if the narration were already haunted by Tyler-laced eruptions from Jack's volatile subconsciousness. We do not believe that we can understand the overall film narration as a representation from the inside, as it were, of Jack's actual hallucinated memories of his history with Tyler, but, as these last examples illustrate, the narration is repeatedly ruptured by outcroppings from Jack's imagination and memory. In this fashion, the movie's narration subtly hints at the larger strategy of non-transparency that it so cunningly constructs.

Part II. The ethics of Fight Club

Another type of twist

Thus far we have focused on the nature of narrative transparency and its specific uses in Fight Club – on the fact that much of what we imagine seeing, at least on first viewing the film, comes to be challenged by our eventual appreciation of Jack's psychological predicament. There is no doubting the centrality of this project of epistemic deflection to the film's overall conception. But we will now suggest that there is a deeper point to this lack of narrative transparency. For at the center of the film is a thematic twist, and this twist parallels the narrative one. The remainder of the essay will be an attempt to diagnose the precise nature and import of this twist.

As we hope to show, understanding the film's subversion of our initially plausible assumptions about its worldview is crucial if we hope to interpret it in a fair and accurate way. Unfortunately, one of the most fascinating things about Fight Club is the frequency with which it is radically *misinterpreted*. This fact has been overshadowed in critical discussions and probably popular discussions as well by interest in the film's epistemic structure; but it is important, in analyzing it, to recall that what many viewers take away from Fight Club has little or nothing to do with the lack of transparency that constitutes the major part of its narrative innovation. What these viewers take from the movie is a certain message, a message that's expressed in the angry diatribes of Tyler Durden, the cathartic pummeling of the clandestine fights, and, at its culmination, in the proto-anarchism of Project Mayhem.

Clearly the film sets up some expectations in this connection. It confronts us with a protagonist whose spiritual predicament is a kind of postmodern malaise that induces a depressed insomnia, and that is apparently linked to the proliferation of consumerism, corporate capitalism, and the resultant emasculation of the American male. Moreover, the film initially appears to deliver to its protagonist a savior, an agent of masculine resurrection, whose central qualities are his sado-masochistic impulses and his unimpeachable virility. So for a while, Fight Club might indeed look like a relatively contrived exercise in adolescent ideology, a glorification of violence and chaos as the only way of rescuing men from the onslaught of modernity and its feminine, domesticating power.[9]

The problem with interpreting the film in this manner is that it quite consciously calls all these ideas into question. One of our aims here will be to show that its subversion of our initial interpretive assumptions is quite obvious – obvious enough to raise an interesting question about *how* the film could remain so susceptible to misinterpretation.

In broad outline, the view that we will be defending is as follows. A major theme of the film is that Jack's spiritual predicament can only be ameliorated by way of the establishment of some sort of real human connection. Initially, it seems as if Tyler is the person who can give him this kind of connection. More generally, the worldview that Tyler espouses and embodies appears to be presented as one that is substantially correct in its diagnosis of, and rebellion against, the emasculated condition of modern man. And the ethos of Tyler is at first portrayed as a viable solution to some distinctively modern problems of meaninglessness, alienation, and homogeneity, problems for which Jack is the film's representative sufferer.

Nonetheless, this conception of the themes of the film is completely mistaken. In our view, Fight Club should leave viewers with the impression that Tyler's worldview is deeply twisted, disturbed, and unproductive. More importantly, viewers should appreciate that this worldview is certainly not presented, at the end of the day, as a legitimate solution to the existential predicament that is the movie's main focus. The connection that Jack seems to have with Tyler, and that seems to be a way of steering him back to psychological normality, is completely illusory – both a figment of his imagination and a red herring in his search for a cure. Ultimately we come to understand that Tyler is really an unhealthy projection of Jack's anger and isolation rather than a prophetic trumpeter of a return to unrestrained masculinity. Furthermore, we'll show that Marla Singer, who occupies a place in Jack's troubled consciousness that is starkly contrasted with the place occupied by Tyler, is actually the film's suggested solution to the problems it treats.[10] More generally, the lesson of Fight Club is one that directly opposes the worldview of Tyler: only real human connection, in the form of run of the mill relationships, engaged feelings, and the capacity for love, can constitute a healthy response to isolation, boredom, and disengagement.

A sketch of the argument

As we've noted, a fairly common conception of the thematic ambitions of Fight Club represents the film as primarily concerned with offering a critique of modern society and, in particular, a critique of modernity's sterilization of certain characteristically masculine impulses. The central idea seems to be that Jack's condition is at least substantially the result of socio-economic factors – such as corporate specialization and rampant, blind consumerism – over which he exercises little control and for which he has no responsibility. It is the return to a more primitive state, one in which men habitually indulge their natural drives, that the film supposedly recommends.

We'll now present our reasons for thinking that this common view of the film is clearly misguided. For simplicity's sake it will be useful to have a name for this interpretive perspective. We will call it the *emasculation model*, but we trust that readers will not accord this title too much significance.

These reasons will be provided by way of an argument that takes us from an analysis of the central narrative developments of Fight Club to a conclusion about the filmmakers' intentions and the fundamental worldview that these intentions exhibit. The argument will serve to highlight just how simply the emasculation model can be called into question, and consequently bring to the fore some important issues about what grounds its appeal, issues about which we will refrain from offering what would inevitably be unscientific speculations. Our main criticism of the emasculation model is that it cannot square with the way *Fight Club's* narrative is conceived. It is only if we overlook some rudimentary facts about the film's structure that this interpretation could appear correct.

Let us first put the argument in a relatively general form. The film sets up a *central problem* for its protagonist. It gives us clues about the nature of this problem, and, in particular, provides us with a *manifestation* of the problem, which presumably functions to illuminate its nature. Then the protagonist finds an *initial possible solution*, a solution that is quickly frustrated and proven inadequate. Eventually, he discovers a *second possible solution*. The second solution is importantly related, as one might expect, to the central problem and to the first, failed response. Our task as interpreters is to evaluate the viability of the second solution – how the filmmakers present it to us, and what their judgments about it seem to be. The view we take to be obvious is that the second solution is portrayed as just as inadequate as the first. And if this is right, then the emasculation model is completely misconceived.

An interpretation of Fight Club

We now articulate the argument in more detail. The central problem of the narrative is Jack's spiritual malaise. After the film's opening, as we flash back to the beginning of the events it depicts, we encounter him as a depressed corporate drone who gets his minimal kicks envisioning possible redecorations of his apartment, contemplating questions like "what kind of dining set defines me as a person?" The source of his condition is not entirely clear.[11] In our view, it is by evaluating the proposed solutions to his problem that we can best understand what the problem is. But the crucial piece of information that we get is that Jack's condition has one chief manifestation: insomnia.

Jack's insomnia is presented as a genuine metaphysical predicament, and not as a simple bout of sleeplessness: "For six months I couldn't sleep. With insomnia nothing's real. Everything is far away. Everything is a copy of a copy of a copy." Early on, then, we are given to understand that the core of his insomnia is not exhaustion but estrangement from reality.

Jack's preliminary reaction to his situation is an interesting one, and viewers often under-appreciate its importance.[12] Following a probably facetious recommendation from his doctor, who is dismissive of Jack's request for sleeping pills and of his claims that he is experiencing real pain, our protagonist begins to attend group therapy meetings for individuals with serious medical conditions like testicular cancer, feigning illness himself. He spends hours each night listening to the tragic stories of victims, hearing about their disappointments and anguish, and even hugging them and engaging in arguably ritualistic acts of affection. His very first meeting includes a transformational one on one encounter: "Strangers with this kind of honesty make me go a big rubbery one . . . [Bob: Go ahead Cornelius, you can cry.] And then something happened. I let go, lost in oblivion, dark and silent and complete. I found freedom. Losing all hope was freedom. [Cut to Jack sleeping.] Babies don't sleep this well." The emotional engagement that Jack finds in the therapy sessions is addicting. He feels "resurrected" each night; he feels loved and made an essential part of a community. Thus the initial solution highlights an *inability to feel*, and an *inability to engage with others* – or, at least, the persistent lack of feeling and emotional engagement that he experiences in the course of his daily life – as essential components of Jack's disturbed psychology. For the progress that Jack makes in these scenes is clearly linked to his renewed emotional engagement with other human beings, even though it takes place in so strange and fabricated a setting.

Quickly,[13] however, the success of the group therapy sessions is disrupted by the appearance of Marla, a dark, mysterious, and disturbed woman who suddenly comes to frequent the circuit of "groups." Her presence is a catastrophe for Jack, about which he's explicit: "If I did have a tumor I would name it Marla. Marla, the little scratch on the roof of your mouth that would heal if only you would stop tonguing it, but you can't."

Why is Marla's appearance so problematic for Jack? Because she forces him to face the artificiality of his conduct – the fact that his attendance at these meetings is not such a big step forward from the "copy" essence of his insomniac malaise. If the root of his ennui is an emotional disconnection, an estrangement from the world and the rest of its inhabitants, then the first attempt we see him make of forging some kind of connection is fraught with duplicity, cynicism, and laziness. If it does work to some degree, for a while, then this is simply preliminary evidence of Jack's extreme psychological debilitation.

Marla's presence is like the presence of an undistorted mirror. Nothing cloaks the absurdity of her attendance; on the contrary, Marla flaunts the fact that she doesn't belong at the groups, showing up to testicular cancer meetings and smoking the whole way through. She is the necessary catalyst for Jack's, and the audience's, first major realization: that the therapy circuit is insufficient treatment for his condition.[14]

Shortly after[15] Marla begins attending the meetings, Jack unwittingly embarks on a second attempt at responding to his condition. This attempt occupies the center of the film's narrative development and the locus of its controversy. To put it succinctly we could say that the second solution is Tyler Durden – who, as we eventually come to understand, is a projection of Jack's own troubled consciousness. More accurately, the second solution is a whole constellation of phenomena inspired by Jack's mental deterioration: Tyler himself, Fight Club, and eventually Project Mayhem.

Before providing a more detailed analysis of these central aspects of the film's thematic architecture, it will be useful to observe how nicely the first half hour of Fight Club brings Jack's possibilities into focus. At the conclusion of this first act, in which we have been introduced to the protagonist, his problems, an initial attempted resolution of them, and an apparent foil in the guise of a deranged femme fatale, we meet a new character, a man who exudes from his very pores a vitality that makes him a perfect contrast to Jack, Marla, and the therapy participants.[16] This section of the film comes to a close with the revelation that Jack's apartment has exploded in a fireball, destroying all of his possessions and leaving him homeless; only later do we realize that this is the first[17] eruption of the Tyler persona. Now Jack is faced with a new predicament: he needs somewhere to go. His doorman asks him if he has someone he can call. He has two people, and, we are led to believe, only two: Marla and Tyler. He calls Marla but hangs up, too afraid to speak with her. And then he calls Tyler. Outside of the bar where they meet, Tyler goads Jack, who cannot bring himself to even a modest level of intimacy after three pitchers of beer, into explicitly asking whether he can stay at his place. Then Tyler asks Jack to hit him as hard as he can.

Here are the beginnings of Jack's flirtation with violence as a route to intimacy and emotional engagement. As the Fight Club develops, Jack discovers that he is 'not alone' in feeling the kind of loneliness and depression that can be at least temporarily remedied by a good old-fashioned thrashing:

> This kid from work, Ricky, couldn't remember whether you ordered pens with blue ink or black. But Ricky was a god for ten minutes when he trounced the *maitre d'* at a local food court . . . You weren't alive anywhere like you were there.

The Club is thus represented as both a forum of intimacy and as a cathartic indulgence of masculine power. As the fights continue, Jack gains confidence and self-esteem:

> JACK (WITH CONDESCENSION, LOOKING AT A CALVIN KLEIN AD):   Is that what a man looks like?
>
> TYLER: Self-improvement is masturbation. Now self-destruction . . .

From the perspective of the emasculation model, Tyler is the film's hero and the representative — indeed, the projectionist — of its distinctive sociological critique. It is undoubtedly easy, at first, to take him to be a hero. Besides being extremely handsome, virile, and dryly funny, Tyler spouts his ideas with charismatic vitriol, and, being an outgrowth of Jack's own consciousness, immediately keys into the condition of our protagonist.[18] Moreover, there is a certain Whitmanesque naturalness that gives some of his reflections on the condition of modern man a very attractive, and in a way very American, nostalgia for a different kind of life:

> "God damn it, an entire generation pumping gas, waiting tables; slaves with white collars. Advertising has us chasing cars and clothes, working jobs we hate so we can buy shit we don't need. We're the middle children of history, man. No purpose or place. We have no Great War. No Great Depression. Our Great War's a spiritual war. Our Great Depression is our lives. We've all been raised on television to believe that one day we'd all be millionaires, and movie gods, and rock stars. But we won't. And we're slowly learning that fact. And we're very, very pissed off.

In the world I see you're stalking elk through the damp canyon forests around the ruins of Rockefeller Center. You'll wear leather clothes that will last you the rest of your life. You'll climb the wrist-thick kudzu vines that wrap the Sears Tower. And when you look down, you'll see tiny figures pounding corn, laying strips of venison on the empty car pool lane of some abandoned superhighway."

Many viewers will sympathize with elements of Tyler's objections to modern corporate hegemony, specialization, and consumerism. And this is precisely where *Fight Club* attains a temporary lack of thematic transparency that parallels its narrative twist. If we find ourselves attracted to Tyler, and to his ethic of mischief and mayhem, then it is partially because we have yet to see where it leads. Tyler's rebellion is relatively innocent as long as it appears to be just a matter of liposuction soap and pornographic splicing into film reels – though of course it is less than fully *masculine*, in the stereotype of Jack's projection, precisely because it has not yet become unrestrained.[19]

The progression of this rebellion, which is ultimately Jack's revolt against himself, forms the major part of the film. It can be seen as a steadily increasing exhibition of the stereotypically masculine characteristics that Jack feels himself to lack. First, Tyler begins sleeping with Marla – expertly, as one would expect, and publicly enough to mock Jack's own sexual abilities. The origin of this affair is illustrative. Marla reaches out to Jack, calling him in a depressed, drugged, and possibly suicidal daze, but Jack ignores her, literally leaving the phone off the hook and walking away as she talks. Tyler – that part of Jack who is not too scared to engage with a woman – picks up where the more timid and apathetic man left off. Jack is angry when he finds out about Tyler and Marla, but he doesn't comprehend his own jealousy, and he directs it at Marla rather than at his own emotional incompetence and mental impairment. ("She invaded my support groups; now she'd invaded my home.") These issues are so monumental that Jack can sleep with Marla not merely without realizing that he is sleeping with her, but also while simultaneously envisioning himself the victim of the noise pollution that Tyler's conquest produces. This intense fragmentation and isolated compartmentalization of Jack's psyche must be taken as an indication of the extreme difficulties he is having with even the sexual side of emotional connection – in other words as exacerbation, and not relief, of his central problem.

Curiously, Jack's crippling inability to diagnose what is going on in his own mind is broken on one early occasion. In a substantially overlooked confession he comments: "If only I'd wasted a couple of minutes and gone to watch Marla Singer die, none of this would have happened." What he means is that, had he engaged with Marla when she wanted and needed it, rather than shying away and letting Tyler deal with her in his place, the downward spiral of Tyler's dominance, his control over Jack's psyche, might have been prevented. Notice how this one small statement, made in voiceover narration and impossible to interpret on a first viewing of the film, actually demonstrates some of the most general and contentious features of the interpretation we are building up. Jack recognizes, at least in some inchoate way, the importance of Marla to his own well being; more generally, he understands the dangers of his emotional paralysis, and the fact that Tyler and his schemes are somehow connected to it; and he hints at the eventually corrosive development of Tyler's influence, and his regrets about facilitating it.

If sleeping with Marla is the first conquest of Tyler's masculine energy, the escalation of the impulses behind Fight Club constitutes its steady culmination. The Club's expansion, and Tyler's burgeoning fame and power, lead him to conduct a series of increasingly insane, anarchic, and immoral activities. To begin with, Tyler orders the members of Fight Club to start random public fights with strangers.[20] He then hands out "assignments" in sealed envelopes, unleashing a secret campaign of destructive shenanigans. Though these designs are far from innocent, it is still not too hard to laugh them off, since they all have a whiff of playfulness. But when Tyler cruelly threatens a convenience store clerk at gunpoint we begin to apprehend the sickness of his worldview.[21]

Finally, the unleashed aggression and strange fraternal camaraderie of Fight Club, and the power high that Tyler feels as a result of his role as creator of this underground phenomenon, give birth to Project Mayhem, a more ambitious exercise in chaos and destruction. Our first understanding of the nature of this project is provided by the hazing ritual that its "applicants" undergo: standing outside the Paper Street house for three days without food or water, they are told that they are too young, ugly, or fat to "train," and subjected to furious verbal abuse. And this is not the only way in which the clan represents an ironic homogenization of the great wild masculinity Tyler had once hoped to unleash with Fight Club. As Project Mayhem grows, we see that its members are forced to shave their heads, wear uniforms, and perform menial tasks while their comfortable leader shouts his anti-individualist aphorisms into a megaphone: "You are not special. You are not a beautiful or unique snowflake. You are the same decaying organic matter as everything else." Moreover, the participants in Project Mayhem, and Jack most of all, have little idea what they are working towards. "Why was Tyler building an army? To what purpose? For what greater good? In Tyler we trusted . . ."

And observe that as the organization's ambitions escalate, Jack responds with a renewed anger and frustration.[22] This anger, which should be seen as a heightened return to his original spiritual malaise, is surely the product of his increasing estrangement from Tyler's plans; it is thus a response to the slowly dawning realization that Tyler is not who Jack hoped he would be. The fact that Tyler shuts Jack out of the development of Project Mayhem signals two things. First, it shows that Tyler has become, over time, an even more independently functioning part of Jack's catastrophic psychological reality. Second, and correlatively, it shows that this part of Jack is more and more a part with which he does not identify. We shouldn't be surprised that this situation, and the climactic car accident that serves as an initial coda to Tyler and Jack's confrontation, spawns a mental breakthrough of sorts, precipitating Tyler's disappearance and Jack's gradual awakening to his own condition. As he ceases to identify with Tyler's plans, and even comes to a vague kind of philosophical opposition to Tyler himself, Jack begins to achieve the kind of separation that is the first stage of his convalescence – the most obvious signs of this change being his frank (if one-sided) conversation with Marla about Tyler outside the "soap factory" that Paper Street has become, and his horror at the death of Bob and his associates' plans to bury him in the garden.[23]

This opposition reaches its apex in the film's final minutes. In the revelation scene, when Tyler appears and coaxes Jack into an understanding of their essential connection, he also indicates that Marla knows too much about them and is a dangerous liability.[24] But far from agreeing with Tyler's suggestion that they get rid of her, Jack tracks her down; offers an apology; confesses, in a direct way, that he has feelings for her; and all but forces her out of town to safety. Then Jack attempts to foil Tyler's signature plot, the arch-project of his worldview: an all-out attack on the credit system. When this becomes impossible, Jack commits an act of partial suicide, shooting himself through the cheek and succeeding in "killing" Tyler. This accomplished, he is able to tell Marla, who on Tyler's orders has been captured and brought to him, that everything will be fine. The film concludes with Jack's most engaged lines of dialogue: "You met me at a very strange time in my life."

Here is a good place to summarize the relatively complicated evolution of Jack's psyche and its place in the film's thematic conception. As we've made clear, Jack's condition at the outset is one of emotional estrangement from reality and especially from other human beings. His first attempt at connection is foiled – ostensibly by Marla, but really by its own cynicism and vacuity. Though Marla herself represents his best possible avenue of connection and his best chance at some semblance of a normal human relationship, Jack is too immature, depressed, and disturbed to appreciate this. Tyler comes to represent the unleashed fountain of Jack's rage at his own predicament and at the world that has consigned him to it. But our appreciation of Tyler, who embodies a proposed *response* to the central problem, changes dramatically: at first, he is apparently a representative of vitality and a return to a more natural, healthy state of being; later, he comes to embody a misanthropic, anti-individualistic, and morally reprehensible pessimism.

Jack's plunge into the Tyler persona is a step away from emotional reality and normality in two respects. First, it involves the creation of an imaginary being who is the channel of Jack's own desires, and who allows Jack to indulge those desires without necessarily confronting them. Second, the kind of engagement with others that Tyler ultimately counsels is a deeply troubling one with which Jack does not ultimately identify. This breakdown between Jack and Tyler causes the termination of Jack's projection – which at first is like another estrangement, and a painful one – that forces him into an awareness of the depth of his own sickness. So if Tyler is a response to the problem of Jack's malaise, it is natural to view the film as an extended exploration of the inadequacy of this response.[25]

We have argued that Jack's problem is his isolation, his inability to connect with other people in any substantial way; and that Tyler is the ultimately unhealthy crystallization of his anger at this problem. The Fight Club should be seen as a beefed up version of group therapy: a ritual celebration of pain, of feeling, which ultimately gets perverted into the cultish worship of some opaque social ideal. Both attempts share an obsession with pain and suffering as the route to recapturing the emotional engagement that is the only cure for Jack's malaise. What the

Fight Club adds is a philosophy of rage – rage at a world that strips men of their natural virility. Anger and pain are, when it comes down to it, the foundational virtues of Tyler's worldview.[26] But the most plausible interpretation of *Fight Club* sees the film as critiquing Tyler's solution, his fetish for anger and pain. Eventually the full operation of the Tyler persona produces a politicization of these emotions that is of little merit. More importantly, it is clear that the culmination of Tyler's worldview – that is, destruction and vaguely socialist anarchism – *cannot* be a viable solution to Jack's problem, and that Jack recognizes this fact. So whatever we think of the politics of Project Mayhem, there should be no question that it, and the whole Tyler experiment of which it forms just one part, is a failed cure for our troubled protagonist.

It is essential to note that the role of women in the life of men is certainly one of the implicit themes of this whole progression. The Fight Club and Project Mayhem are purely masculine enterprises, and they constitute inadequate responses to the problem of the film. At one point Tyler remarks, in speaking of marriage, "We're a generation of men raised by women. I wonder if another woman is really what we need."

For some time, it may be reasonable to think of the movie as genuinely concerned with the excessive femininity of modern man. But this is not the impression that we should have by the end of the film. *Contra* the emasculation model, the lesson of *Fight Club* is not that modernity has stripped men of their natural virility, and that reclaiming it is the only road to a renewed psychological equilibrium. Really the film's worldview is far more conventional. There is no doubt that some of its criticisms of corporate life and global capitalism are in earnest. Jack's spiritual condition, however, is not traceable solely to these external forces. As Tyler says, he needs to take some responsibility. His condition is most fundamentally a matter of his disturbing estrangement from other people, and, in particular, his incapacity to engage with a woman who almost inexplicably finds him interesting. The ending of the film is hopeful precisely because Jack has finally come to appreciate this simple truth, and the strange woman who has taught it to him.

Notes

1   George Wilson acknowledges the following: earlier versions of the first half of this essay were read at the 2004 meetings of the American Society for

Aesthetics in Houston and at departmental colloquia at both the University of Southern California and the University of California at Riverside. The final version has benefited from each of these occasions. Among the people whose comments were especially helpful to him are William Bracken, David Davies, Berys Gaut, John Martin Fisher, Janet Levin, Jerry Levinson, Katalin Makkai, Michael Renov, Dana Polan, Murray Smith, Gideon Yaffee, Tom Wartenberg, and Gareth Wilson. Both of us are especially indebted to Karen Wilson, who made crucial points to each of us. Sam Shpall would also like to thank Jillian Bleiweiss and Barker Gerard.

2 A further interesting example is given in Flory (2011).

3 However, there have been important systematic discussions of the topic in earlier literature. For example, see Mitry (1977); Kawin (1978); and Branigan (1984).

4 Walton (1997) argues for this thesis in "On Pictures and Photographs: Objections Answered" and Wilson (1997) argues for it in "*Le Grand Imagier* Steps Out: On the Primitive Basis of Film Narration."

5 It is not simply that this scenario is something we can imagine. It is a scenario that is actually depicted in an episode of the old British television series, *The Prisoner*. The episode is called "A, B, & C," and it was directed by Pat Jackson and written by Anthony Skene, ITV1 (UK), October 15, 1967. We owe this reference to Steve Reber and Geoff Georgi.

6 See Mitry (1997), pp. 214–19. Mitry gives an example from *Jezebel* (William Wyler, 1938) that is similar to the somewhat more complicated one we describe.

7 The aptness of this shot for our purposes was suggested by Deborah Thomas's discussion in *Reading Hollywood: Spaces and Meanings in American Film*. See Thomas (2001), pp.102–5. Despite appearances, this is not a tracking shot. It was made by a stationary camera on a revolving platform, as discussed by Auiller (1998).

8 Although the character is nameless in *Fight Club*, it has become standard in the literature on the film to refer to him as "Jack" for reasons that are obvious enough in the movie.

9 For two of the more hyperbolic, though representative, criticisms of the film on this score, see Kenneth Turan (Review of *Fight Club* in the *Los Angeles Times*: October 14, 1999): "Though the film employs dubious plot twists to quasi-distance itself from the weirder implications of a philosophy the Columbine gunmen would likely have found congenial, it's to little effect"; and Henry A. Giroux ("Private Satisfactions and Public Disorders: *Fight Club*, Patriarchy, and the Politics of Masculine Violence." *Journal of Advanced Composition* 21.1 (Spring 2001): 1–31): "*Fight Club* defines the violence of capitalism almost exclusively in terms of an attack on traditional (if not to say regressive) notions of masculinity, and in doing so reinscribes white heterosexuality within a dominant logic of stylized brutality and male bonding that appears predicated on the need to denigrate and wage war against all that is feminine."

Gary Crowdus (*Cineaste* 25.4 (September 2000): 47) summed up the immediate critical reception: "While Fight Club had numerous critical champions, the film's critical attackers were far more vocal, a negative chorus which became hysterical about what they felt to be the excessively graphic scenes of fisticuffs ... They felt such scenes served only as a mindless glamorization of brutality, a morally irresponsible portrayal, which they feared might encourage impressionable young male viewers to set up their own real-life fight clubs in order to beat each other senseless." Janet Maslin, in the *New York Times* (October 15, 1999) was one of the critics to suggest the sentiment that we will be defending in what follows: "If watched sufficiently mindlessly, it might be mistaken for a dangerous endorsement of totalitarian tactics and super-violent nihilism in an all-out assault on society."

10   *Contra* the claims of some critics, who regard Marla as a "cipher for male sexual fantasies, fears, and inadequacies" (Hooper, Charlotte. "Fighting Offers No Real Redemption." *International Feminist Journal of Politics* 4.1 (April 2002): 131–32); as "in sum the object in the most basic and stereotypical type of male fantasy" (Carver, Terrell. "*Fight Club*: Dramma Giocosa." *International Feminist Journal of Politics* 4.1 (April 2002): 129–31); and as having "no identity outside of the needs of the warrior mentality" (Giroux 18).

11   At the outset, the film suggests a strong link between the corporate homogeneity of Jack's existence and his alienation and boredom. Tyler gives us a more developed picture of this interpretation, and we think that the filmmakers are definitely concerned to present this kind of social critique to some degree. The question is whether they want to indicate that these are the main causes of Jack's illness. In our view, the root of his problem is a psychological and moral deficiency that cannot be attributed to the existence of furniture stores and insurance corporations.

12   It is telling and ironic that the segments of the film most overlooked by proponents of the emasculation view are those whose importance can only be understood by appealing to the role of the lone female lead. In a moment we will see that Marla's appearance is the death-knell for Jack's first redemption fantasy.

13   Interestingly, Jack tells us that he has been attending the meetings, and apparently sleeping well, for a full year; and we also discover that Tyler has been living in the house on Paper Street for a year. So it might be that the apparent progress from the meetings has been a *total* illusion – the Tyler persona has been steadily germinating the whole time – and Marla has merely brought this into partial view.

14   Two passages in the script are especially illustrative:

JACK: Marla. The big tourist. Her lie reflected my lie. Suddenly I felt nothing. I couldn't cry. So once again, I couldn't sleep.

And their confrontational exchange:

JACK:	You're a tourist . . . I saw you at melanoma, tuberculosis, and testicular cancer.
MARLA:	I saw you practicing this . . .
JACK:	Practicing what?
MARLA:	Telling me off. Is it going as well as you hoped? *Rupert?*
JACK:	I'll expose you.
MARLA:	I'll expose *you.*

15 At least in terms of the film's superficial chronology. See note 13.

16 This sense of opposition is clearly cultivated. In his first major scene, on the plane, Tyler wears sunglasses, a red checked blazer, and plaid slacks, and nonchalantly slips his way into the restricted captain's area without anyone (including most first-time viewers) noticing what he's doing. Moments later he is stealing a red convertible from the curb at the airport terminal.

17 We should note again here that the chronology of the film's events is very difficult to ascertain with certainty. It could be argued that the explosion of Jack's apartment takes place towards the end of his year-long engagement with Tyler, and perhaps that it is the genesis of Project Mayhem. On this picture, the Tyler persona has been operating independently for quite some time before Jack actually "meets" him on the airplane.

18 It is noteworthy that some of his opening words to Jack are, first, echoes of Marla (Jack asks him what he does and Tyler says "Why, so you can pretend like you're interested," just as Marla has, in the confrontation scene, justified her coming to the meetings by invoking the way normal people merely talk to hear themselves); and, second, evidence of an instant comprehension of his spiritual anguish ("You have a kind of sick desperation in your laugh"). Marla, who because she is an actual person does not have this kind of instant comprehension, represents Jack's real chance to address his issues in a constructive way. The idea that human relationships could be essentially a matter of telepathy is just as indicative of Jack's sickness as his satisfaction with the inauthentic engagement of the "groups."

19 These early sections of the film are at pains to paint Tyler's indulgences in a comic light: "Tyler sold his soap to department stores at $20 a bar. God knows what they charged . . . It was beautiful. We were selling rich women their own fat asses back to them."

20 Jack executes this order by feigning a fight with his boss as an elaborate, and ultimately successful, attempt at bribery. Pummeling himself in his office, he notes that "for some reason, I thought of my first fight with Tyler." In retrospect, we know that he has a very good reason: on both occasions he is fighting himself. It is Jack's severance that funds Fight Club and Project Mayhem.

21 Jack does too: he "feels ill" and doesn't see the point of this cruel display. But when Tyler tells Jack that the clerk's breakfast the next day will taste better than any meal either of them have ever had, Jack comes to see the point, and

admires the fact that Tyler always has a "plan" that "makes sense in a Tyler sort of way." Again, Jack is intoxicated to the point of impairment by Tyler's power and foreignness.

22   Cf. his fight against the blonde initiate (played by Jared Leto), in which he brutalizes the young man to a degree unacceptable in Fight Club. In response to Tyler's disappointment Jack says that he "felt like destroying something beautiful."

23   The depth of the brainwashing that we see at work in Project Mayhem should not be underestimated. When Jack says to the men that the dead man is a friend of his, who has a name, his underlings understand this as a symbol: in death, a member acquires the name that he lacked in life. But it is clear that a cult of death is not what Jack longed for in the midst of his insomnia and depression. And it is certainly not what he found attractive about Tyler, who initially began as a poet of unrestrained vitality.

24   As Karen Wilson has pointed out to us, Tyler seems to be wearing Marla's fur coat, or at least a very similar one, in this important scene. Perhaps this is meant to be a further indication that Jack's psychological compartmental-ization is breaking down, and that Marla is, as he suspects, the key to his understanding and recovery.

25   Perhaps Tyler says it best: "You were looking for a way to change your life. You could not do this on your own. All the ways you wish you could be- that's me." Of course, Tyler is an example of Jack attempting to sort things out on his own. That's why he can't be a realistic solution to the problem of engaging with others.

26   Cf. the soap-making scene, in which Tyler puts the unsuspecting Jack through a trial of burning chemical agony. When Jack tries to shut out the pain Tyler berates him: "This is your pain, this is your burning hand, it's right here . . . this is the greatest moment of your life, man, and you're off somewhere missing it." Note that when Jack attempts to escape into a fantasy of his own instinctive design, one of his constructed images includes Marla, supine and receiving his kisses.

Works cited

Auiller, Dan. 1998. *Vertigo: The Making of a Hitchcock Classic*. New York: St. Martin's Press.

Branigan, Edward. 1984. *Point of View in Film*. Berlin: Mouton Publishers.

Flory, Dan. 2011. "Cinematic Presuppositions, Race, and Epistemological Twist Films." In *The Journal of Aesthetics and Art Criticism* 68: 379–88.

Kawin, Bruce. 1978. *Mindscreen*. Princeton, NJ: Princeton University Press.

Mitry, Jean. 1977. *The Aesthetics and Psychology of the Cinema* (C. King, Trans.). Bloomington: Indiana University Press.

Thomas, Deborah. 2001. *Reading Hollywood: Spaces and Meanings in American Film*. London: Wallflower.

Walton, Kendall. 1997. "On Pictures and Photographs: Objections Answered." In R. Allen and M. Smith (eds.), Film Theory and Philosophy. Oxford: Clarendon Press.

Wilson, George. 1997. "Le Grand Imagier Steps Out: On the Primitive Basis of Film Narration." In Philosophical Topics 25: 295–318.

Some suggested further reading

Cynthia Kuhn and Lance Rubin, Reading Chuck Palahniuk: American Monsters and Literary Mayhem (London: Routledge, 2009). Several of the essays in this collection discuss the film version of Fight Club.

Jean Mitry, The Aesthetics and Psychology of the Cinema. Trans. by Christopher King (Bloomington: Indiana University Press, 1997). One of the great classics of film theory, this book contains one of the earliest studies of "subjectivity" in film representation.

Chuck Palahniuk, Fight Club: A Novel (New York: W.W. Norton, 1996). The differences between the book and the film are instructive in relation to the topics discussed in the present essay.

Murray Smith, Engaging Characters: Fiction, Emotion, and the Cinema (Oxford: Clarendon Press, 1995). A careful, illuminating investigation of the various ways in which "identification" is a key component of a film viewer's engagement with a movie story and its characters.

Kendall Walton, Mimesis as Make Believe (Cambridge: Harvard University Press, 1990). One of the great classics of contemporary aesthetics. It introduces the idea that "imagined seeing" is critical to our experience of the visual arts generally and to our experience of fiction film in particular.

Chapter 6

Nancy Bauer

THE FIRST RULE OF FIGHT CLUB: ON PLATO, DESCARTES, AND *FIGHT CLUB*[1]

O F WHAT USE ARE FILMS for philosophy? Of philosophy for film? You would think, from perusing textbooks and course syllabi, that films are useful to the philosopher, and to the teacher of philosophy, insofar as they *illustrate* philosophical problems or positions. Take the obvious example of *The Matrix* (dir. Andy and Lana Wachowski, 1999). Philosophers love it, not because it is a film masterwork but because it dramatizes the potential real-life stakes of the "problem of the external world" version of philosophical skepticism, specifically its "brain in a vat" variation. For the student initiate, reading Descartes or Hilary Putnam – or even a potted textbook summary of their views – is unlikely to be as gripping or thought-provoking as watching a horrified Keanu Reeves as he comes to inhabit his "real" self in a huge farm of envatted human beings. The hope is that the film's engagement of human passions will get viewers more interested in certain standing philosophical concerns. And to the extent that students start to perceive philosophical concerns in the films they view, the value of these films will extend beyond the mere capacity to entertain.

Contesting this attenuated way of understanding the relationship between philosophy and film has been a lifelong project of Stanley Cavell's. What fundamentally links the two enterprises, Cavell has argued over the last 40 years, is the extent to which film, by virtue of its nature as a medium and as a matter of historical fact, tends to be preoccupied with philosophy's preoccupations.[2] That films, in their explorations of these preoccupations, are often able to rouse passions where philosophy does not, is for Cavell not a brute pedagogical fact but a reason to explore exactly why and how they succeed in doing so. An intimately related question for Cavell, one that drives all of his work, is the relationship passions have to reason. Professional philosophy these days is apt to follow Kant's increasingly influential lead and identify reason as whatever is left of the human mind once the passions are excluded. But films by their nature relentlessly – you might even say absolutely – resist this picture. How and why they do so, Cavell finds, is not something one can discover apart from careful criticism of individual movies – what he calls "reading" films.

Following Cavell's lead, I want here at least to begin a reading of David Fincher's *Fight Club*, released in 1999. What's of particular interest to me about this film is the way that it develops a vision of the intimate relationship between reason and passion in terms that appear to have been lifted from the work of two philosophers whose work turns on denying this relationship – one of them, Descartes, the quintessential modern philosopher, and the other, Plato, its avatar in the ancient world. I will be arguing that *Fight Club*'s challenge to the Cartesian and Platonic pictures takes the form of its figuring its protagonist's failure to know how things really are in the world as a function of his avoidance of his own passions.[3] But before I can try to make the case for this claim, I need to give a more detailed account of my concerns with the mainstream understanding of how philosophy and film mutually inform each other and to spend some time getting my understanding of the Cartesian and Platonic pictures on the table. This account and understanding are products not just of my experience of philosophical texts, but also of what I have learned from multiple viewings of *Fight Club* and other films that take up a similar set of preoccupations. I hope to show why it's not an accident that film and philosophy share these (among other) preoccupations, and how and why I take film's contribution to the discussion to do way more than merely provide illustrations for it.

I. Professing philosophy, professing film studies

Film's resistance to Plato's and Descartes's general conception of reason and its relation to passion, a resistance I find to be epitomized in *Fight Club*, is bound to make philosophers of a certain stripe nervous. If passion is exactly what reason is not – if, that is to say, passion is on the side of irrationality – then to the extent that films play on our affective capacities, films must be seen to lie essentially outside of the philosopher's purview. Engaging students' interest by rousing their passions is a dangerous business; once a film shown in class does its job, the task of the philosopher is to bring students safely back over the border, to the side of reason. Famously, Plato in the tenth book of the *Republic* warns that philosopher-kings must banish poetry from their realms; for art, in all its beauty, seduces the hoi polloi away from what philosophy shows us rationality reveals and demands, and it substitutes at best a distorted copy of reality and a suspect vision of what being human demands of us. Contemporary philosophers of course want film to have a place in the culture – only not the central one in the culture's seat of rationality, which of course is to be found, if it is to be found anywhere, in the philosophy classroom. Of course, there are some philosophers who take film to be an object worthy of serious philosophical interest. But these philosophers tend to be centrally focused on making the case that films appeal not "merely," as it were, to human affect but also to rationality – where, of course, the implicit assumption, the one that forestalls most philosophers from taking film seriously as a philosophical medium – is that we've got two distinctly different capacities on our hands here.[4]

Even those philosophers who are willing to concede that whatever line there might be between reason and passion is at best fuzzy are likely to resist Cavell's idea that film is, by its nature, a philosophical medium. For professional philosophy these days is governed by the idea that the business of the discipline, a business that is not at all compatible with the business of art, is to propose theses and construct theories and then employ certain established methods of argumentation to support them. This broadly scientistic understanding of what philosophy is good for represents a decisive rejection of the picture of philosophy that we find, as Cavell has noted, at the inception of the discipline in Plato's early dialogues, in which the work of philosophy takes place literally in the marketplace, where the philosopher, epitomized by the figure of Socrates, undertakes the task not of arguing for or against various positions but of attracting his friends to converse about the assumptions that under-gird and guide their lives.[5] Plato's picture rests on an understanding of philosophy not as an argument-producing machine but as a mode of education, one that depends essentially on the having and trusting of friends. This is a vision of philosophy that, unlike the conventional conception, is at least in principle congenial to the suggestion that film is a medium of philosophy. For the power of both film and, on this vision, of philosophy, can be seen to depend upon our willingness and ability to talk with our acquaintances about what they care about.

But of course competing visions of what philosophy is and does find their parallel in equally competing visions of what film is and does. Professional philosophy's repression of the early Plato is mirrored in the tendency of film scholars to imagine that their job is to construct a priori theories about how movies work on their audiences and then point to this or that film as evidence of the power of the theories. On this top-down conception of how to think about films, one's movie-watching experience – the ways one finds oneself responding to particular films – is fundamentally not to be trusted and indeed inevitably stands in need of criticism via the lens of a theory, the job of which will sometimes be not just to explain the experience but to explain it away. On Laura Mulvey's extremely influential view, for example, the pleasure we derive from narrative films – *all* narrative films, she says – hopelessly and insidiously turns on their inevitable objectification of women and therefore must be disavowed.[6] In questioning the priority that Mulvey assigns to theory in characterizing how we experience all narrative films, one need not insist that viewers are always in control of the way that the movies they watch affect them, or that the effects in question are unadulterated by the movie-watcher's sometimes morally or politically worrisome investments. But we also need not reject the idea that films have the power, on their own, to engage these investments – and, as often as not, to challenge rather than confirm them. What film theory seems to require is the conviction that films are not, as it were, on top of their own powers – that they lack something like a self-consciousness of what they are all about.

In its certainty that film as a medium stands in need of systematic explication – that one's experience of a film cannot, on its own, ground any serious intellectual work – film theory finds what is perhaps an unlikely bedfellow in academic philosophy. The practice of professional philosophy in fact is premised on the idea that experience isn't the source of explanations; to the contrary, it's what stands in need of explaining. We are to dope out How Things Fundamentally Are With the World quite apart from whatever particular experiences we personally may have had. If we make an appeal to our own experience, it is because we require an example of what stands in need of explanation or because we wish to show how our favorite theory happens to get confirmed by experiential evidence. In fact, a film might end up coming in handy in this enterprise; it can dramatize how chaotic raw experience is and how desperately it stands in need of being ordered via a philosophical theory. Take Tim Robbins's film Dead Man Walking (1995), for example. This movie is loosely based on the experiences of Helen Prejean (played in the film by Susan Sarandon), a real-life nun who was forced to learn about both sides of the death-penalty debates when she agreed to serve as the spiritual counselor to a death-row murderer and rapist, played in the film by Sean Penn. A philosophy teacher might screen this movie with the purpose of impressing on students the viability of his decided view that the death penalty is morally execrable – or, perhaps, tolerable or even laudable. The assumption guiding this use of the film is that, because it is "just" a film, it has precisely no independent philosophical import.[7]

This assumption constitutes a denial of my experience of Dead Man Walking, which is that the film aspires to change the terms of the death-penalty debates. It does this, I find, in two principal ways. First, the director, Tim Robbins, uses cutting and framing techniques to dramatize the lengths to which the state goes to protect individuals who carry out death-row executions – and, for that matter, ordinary citizens – from the fact of their own participation in these killings. In numerous point-of-view shots, for example, various prison employees are shown to attend only to very small moments of the condemned man's execution – the strapping down of his arm or the pushing of a button – actions that together add up to "the state's" (and not specific human beings') taking of a human life. These shots and others, I submit, press on us the question of what a state is and what it is for a state to act in the name of citizens it strives to keep completely anonymous as they carry out its business. Second, Robbins uses intercutting to bring to light the difficulty, papered over by the tit-for-tat structure of our punishment system, of comparing the passionlessness and sterility of a state-sanctioned murder with the chaos and savagery of those murders that land people on death row. In my experience, the philosophical interest of Dead Man Walking, a respectable if not brilliant Hollywood movie, lies not in its support or condemnation of the death penalty, though philosophers who comment on it are inclined to reduce it to these terms. Instead, the film draws our attention to features of state-sanctioned killing that have been scarcely articulable in the current death penalty debates. The potential power of even *Dead Man Walking* to change the terms of our conversation points to at least one reason not to regard films as in principle inferior to written philosophical works.

There is another important reason that I am resistant to the project of relegating films in an a priori way to a lower philosophical status than the books and essays that constitute the philosophical canon, but I cannot articulate it without first considering the question of why philosophers are inclined to deny the integrity of films as philosophical texts. This task, it turns out, will require a detour into the history of philosophy, starting with the founding of the modern version of the enterprise in the mid-seventeenth century and working backwards to the roots of the profession in Plato.

II. Descartes and Plato

The text that gets modern philosophy off the ground is Descartes's *Meditations*, which, according to legend was conceived by Descartes after he spent a restless night in an overheated room – a fact I mention only because insomnia will eventually become a central theme of my reading of *Fight Club*. In the *Meditations*, this project is mortally threatened almost immediately: it turns out that its first result is Descartes's finding himself forced to worry that the world as he knows it is a figment of his imagination. He notices, to take things a little more slowly, that all of his experience can be explained just as well by the hypothesis that he is dreaming or that he is being systematically manipulated by an all-powerful demon as by the ordinary idea that a real world, in which he dwells and with which he really interacts, exists. By the end of the first meditation, Descartes is in a panic: does anything at all actually exist? What begins to reassure him of the genuine materiality of the world is the fact of his own thought: no matter how false his understanding of things is, it's still *his* understanding, so at the very least he must exist, at least as a "thinking thing."

After this climactic moment in the *Meditations*, Descartes tries to bring himself back to his senses by convincing himself that his most basic beliefs are underwritten by a perfectly beneficent God, one who would not trap us in our own heads, as it were. Notoriously, however, this proof is considerably less than decisive, so that the most salient legacy of the *Meditations* is an image of a disembodied man who lacks the resources to judge the status of his own experience of the world.[8] Descartes's own term for this state of extreme skepticism about the epistemic reliability of our ordinary experience is "madness." And it could be said that in the 350 years since the publication of the *Meditations*, we philosophers have been trying to regain our sanity. The task of modern philosophy has been to identify and secure the foundations of our ordinary experience – as though by failing to sublime this experience philosophically we are systematically and relentlessly imperiling ourselves.

Before Descartes, during the ancient and medieval periods, philosophers conceived of themselves in the business not of securing the foundations of our knowledge but of describing the world in terms of what they *already* knew to be true – what Homer or the Scriptures, for example, had said. The guiding purpose of philosophical inquiry was not to theorize one's way back from the brink of madness but to propose a grand vision of how to live, and this inquiry took the form of a revaluation of everyday experience. The methodology of philosophy was to bring us to a new vision of our everyday lives, and this point is epitomized in what is perhaps the most famous image in the history of the enterprise: Plato's cave. Since the details of this image are critical to my project, I want to rehearse the way Plato constructs and uses it.

Plato asks us to imagine an underground cave at the bottom of which is a group of prisoners, shackled so that they cannot move their heads and are consigned to face the cave's back wall (see Figure 6.1). Behind these prisoners, Plato says, we are to imagine a ledge (see Figure 6.2) on which other people are manipulating various everyday objects and making corresponding sound effects.

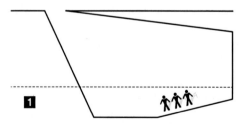

Figure 6.1 The shackled prisoners face the back wall of the cave

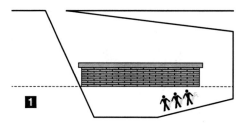

Figure 6.2 The ledge behind the prisoners

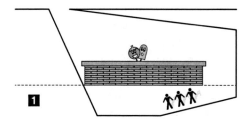

Figure 6.3 Objects being manipulated on the ledge

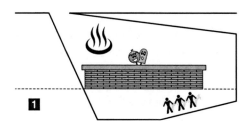

Figure 6.4 The fire behind the ledge, which casts shadows on the prisoners' wall

Behind the ledge there is a huge fire, the light from which casts shadows of the objects being manipulated onto the prisoners' wall (see Figure 6.4). For the prisoners, Plato observes, "reality" will consist exclusively in these shadows.

Now suppose, Plato suggests, that one of the prisoners is unshackled and encouraged to turn around, to set his back to the wall (see Figure 6.5).

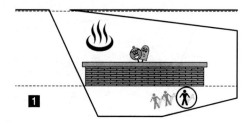

Figure 6.5 One prisoner is unshackled and encouraged to turn around

At first, Plato speculates, the strong light from the fire would blind him, and he would attempt to turn back to what is familiar. But if he were courageous and curious enough, he would not turn back, and gradually his eyes would adjust to the light. Let us imagine, Plato proposes, that this man walks away from his fellow prisoners, towards and then beyond the wall, to the fire.

The "2" in Figure 6.6 is to indicate that, according to Plato, the prisoner now has a new, second perspective on the world. The very existence of this second perspective will of course reveal the first, the one in which reality consists in the shadows on the wall, *as* a perspective itself. You might say that seeing things from the second perspective gives the prisoner a philosophical perspective on the nature of the first. When the prisoner reaches this second place, he will recognize that what he previously took to be real was actually a mere representation of what now appears to be ultimate reality: the ledge, the objects being manipulated on it, and the fire.

Plato now imagines the freed prisoner being encouraged to walk past the ledge, the objects, and the fire, toward the mouth of the cave.

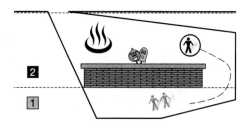

Figure 6.6 The unshackled prisoner walks toward the fire and a second
perspective on reality

Once again, the prisoner will be loathe to leave behind what he takes to be real. And since the light outside the cave will be much brighter even than the light of the fire, he will once again be blinded and will have to overcome the strong urge to turn back. But, if he is blessed with the right temperament, he will bring himself to leave the comfort of the cave (see Figure 6.7).

When his eyes adjust, the former prisoner will discover that what he previously took to be real – the people moving the objects on the ledge in front of the fire – was just so much play-acting: a copying of the real world. This means that what he was originally looking at on the wall was a copy of a copy – a mere piece of art, by the lights of Book X of the *Republic*.

Eventually, Plato suggests, the prisoner may discover in himself the desire and fortitude to look upward and behold the sun, which for Plato represents the realm of pure Ideas and thus the true ultimate reality (see Figure 6.8).

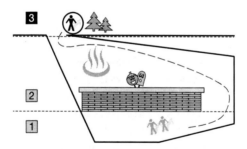

Figure 6.7 The prisoner leaves the cave and gains a third perspective on reality

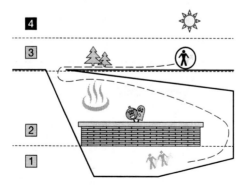

Figure 6.8 The sun, which represents the realm of pure Ideas, the ultimate reality

Now, Plato believed that the things of this world – the things one finds at what I'm identifying as level 3, the things of our everyday lives – are themselves copies of the Ideas emblematized by the sun and accessible (at level 4) only to people well trained in thinking, that is, to philosophers. This means that, from the point of view of the philosopher, what the prisoners at level 1 are viewing is merely a copy of a copy of a copy.

Notice that what Plato conveys via the figure of the cave is not the Cartesian idea that our ordinary experience is unreliable, nor, à la a later version of modern skepticism that we find in Kant, that the truth of how things are with the world – whether or to what extent our experience is drastically limited by the nature of our minds – is in principle beyond our grasp. Rather, what Plato's image suggests is that we, that is to say, the prisoners in the cave, are fixated on the light and shadows the world casts and that to think and live truly we must muster up the courage to turn around and walk away. Let me put this point more provocatively, the way Cavell has taught me to do: Plato is exhorting us to walk out on the feature presentation. His prisoners, hypnotized by the shadows that play on the wall, composing a world out of these effects of artifice, are watching movies (see Figure 6.9).[9]

If we remind ourselves that Plato wished to ban all art from his Republic on the grounds that it entices people away from the hard work of philosophy and drugs them into contentment with mere shadows of reality, we can appreciate Cavell's suggestion that at its founding moment Western philosophy in effect defines itself over and against film, as though delimiting itself by pointing to what it is emphatically not.

The difference between this founding moment and the modern one that Descartes inaugurates is that the moral of the Cartesian story appears to be the impossibility of the turning around Plato recommends to

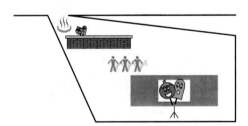

Figure 6.9 The shadows on the wall as movies

us. We are enslaved in our own consciousnesses, consigned either to go on watching the wall of shadows or to shut our eyes. I said earlier that philosophy today continues to be controlled by Cartesian skepticism. I can now put the claim this way: the conditions that define modern philosophy are strikingly similar to the conditions of watching a film. In both cases, the existence of the – or, in the case of film I should probably say "a" – world is at stake. You might think that a major difference here is that the philosopher is desperately trying to *confirm* the existence of the world of his or her ordinary experience, while the filmgoer, as the cliché would have it, willingly suspends disbelief in the world that any decent narrative film conjures up. But Cavell's view is premised on the sense that something like the opposite is true here: our culture's craving for films is a sign of our desperate desire to believe in a vision of the world, and a place for the human in it, while the philosopher's madness results from his developing our uncanny capacity to ward this desire off.

What interests me about *Fight Club* is the way that it studies what you might call this dialectic of desire, the way that it evokes our yearning for a coherent world in which we can invest ourselves, precisely by scrutinizing the resistance to this craving epitomized in the stance of the modern philosopher. *Fight Club* relies on the trope of sleeplessness to map the topography of a certain state of Cartesian madness. It identifies this madness, figured as insomnia, as a state of being unable to feel or express one's emotions. And this apathy is shown to produce a profound separation from other people, one that in effect denies their existence, so that the film ends up implying that the hallmark of Cartesian skepticism is an extreme, violent form of pathological narcissism. *Fight Club* claims, in other words, that the most important legacy of Cartesianism is ethical rather than epistemological.

III: On *Fight Club*

Let's begin with what's uncontroversial. *Fight Club* is the story of an anonymous corporate drone, played by Edward Norton, who begins to suffer from terrible insomnia.[10] His sleeplessness is alleviated only by his sobbing his heart out at all sorts of support groups for diseases he doesn't have – testicular cancer, brain parasites, degenerative bone disease, tuberculosis, organic brain dementia, sickle cell anemia, and on and on. When the protagonist cannot cry, he cannot feel anything; and when he cannot feel anything, he cannot sleep. But when he invades the testicular cancer support group Remaining Men Together, he sleeps, as he puts it, better than a baby. The plot of Fight Club is set in motion by the protagonist's meeting a woman named Marla Singer, played by Helena Bonham Carter, who, just like the protagonist, is a support-group junkie. Marla both deeply attracts and deeply repulses the protagonist in part because her fakery forces him to confront his own. Marla – "the little scratch on the top of your mouth that would heal if only you could stop tonguing it, but you can't," as the protagonist describes her – makes it impossible for the protagonist to cry, hence feel, hence sleep. In the deep state of insomnia that overtakes him as a result, the protagonist meets the seductive Tyler Durden, played by the seductive Brad Pitt, who draws him further and further into violent resistance against the culture that has spawned his meaningless life. At the core of this resistance is a nationwide network of "fight clubs," ever-growing groups of alienated men who get together late at night, when other people are sleeping, in warehouses and industrial basements – so many underground caves – and do what is perhaps most accurately described as beating the shit out of each other. Tyler Durden interprets these men's desperate need to feel something – their collective insomnia, as the film figures it – as a form of socially mandated emasculation. So it's no wonder that his recipe for relief, his way of Remaining Men Together, takes the hyper-masculine form of, at first, giving and receiving punches and, later, all-out acts of terror against corporate America.

Toward the end of Fight Club, we come to learn that Tyler Durden does not exist – or, rather, that his reality is a function of the protagonist's insomnia. When the protagonist drifts off at night and at other moments of extreme exhaustion into a hellish state that's neither wakefulness nor dreaming, Tyler, it turns out, takes over his body. Tyler is Cartesian skepticism distilled to its essence: a personality whose existence is perfectly coextensive with his thinking. And yet, unlike the protagonist, through whose body and voice, we are given to understand, he commands legions of men, Tyler makes himself known to other people – though not to the protagonist, whose recognition of Tyler's true nature lags even behind ours. The protagonist's unwillingness to let others know him is signified in his abiding namelessness, which is underscored by the different pseudonyms he uses on each of his "Hello, my name is . . ." support group badges. "Who are you?" Marla demands when they first confront one another at the beginning of the film. "Cornelius? Rupert? Travis? Any of the names you give yourself each night?" This question of who the narrator is becomes even more urgent for Marla throughout the film, as she commences an affair with (what she does not know to be) the Tyler persona, much to the disgust of the protagonist, whose frightening and utterly confounding contempt for her after her trysts with his alter-ego continually raises worries for her about his identity. Marla, it is revealed at the end of the film, has learned to call the narrator "Tyler," and of course she is not exactly wrong in this practice – just as we are not mistaken when we refer to Brad Pitt in this film as "Tyler." Indeed, I wish to claim, an achievement of this film is the way it invites us to ask what it is that a human being's name names, which is to say, what a human being is.

This question takes its highest form, perhaps, in the film's response to the requirement – demanded by the transformation of Chuck Palahniuk's story into the photographic medium – that the roles of the protagonist and Tyler Durden be played by two different actors. The coherence of the film depends on our accepting at one and the same time (1) that Tyler Durden is a figment of the protagonist's imagination and (2) the presence of Brad Pitt on the screen. The most unnerving moments of the film may well be those in which the contradiction is shoved in our faces, as Pitt, via security cameras within the mise-en-scène, flashbacks, and so forth, seems suddenly to evanesce, and we see Edward Norton punching *himself*. At the heart of this film, then, is the paradox that Brad Pitt's body is an essential part of the film *Fight Club* and yet it does not, cannot, exist. And this paradox doesn't govern just what goes on within the film; it's an essential condition of the possibility of the film itself: there is no Brad Pitt, no human being, literally, in front of us – just lights and shadows cast on a screen in a dark place sealed off from the real world.

But for that matter, the Cartesian in us has to wonder: is there *ever*, even when we imagine we're dealing with the real thing, "literally" a human being in front of us? I've never met the flesh-and-blood Brad Pitt. Is he computer-generated? Is he who he is on screen? Who is Brad Pitt? What does the person who gets paid for Brad Pitt's roles have in common with the figure I have come to know on film as "Brad Pitt"? Suppose the "real" Brad Pitt showed up one day on my doorstep. How could I know with absolute certainty that I wasn't just dreaming him up? These skeptical questions are on the same page as the ones over which philosophers have obsessed for the last several centuries. What *Fight Club* suggests is that this sort of obsession is a cover for a deeper, more human, more passionate question about what it means to recognize another person's existence – and, specifically, in the film's world, the existence of Marla. The achievement of this recognition, or what Cavell would call "acknowledgment," is further shown to require a willingness to allow another person to recognize you, to use your name. The protagonist's willingness for mutual recognition is what eventually kills off Tyler Durden, what brings the protagonist back from the limbo between being asleep and being awake. What fosters this willingness?

Let us return, for an answer, to an early moment in the movie, at which the protagonist identifies insomnia with the condition of the prisoners in Plato's cave, which is to say, as I've suggested, with the watching of a film: "With insomnia," he says, "nothing's real. Everything's far away. Everything's a copy of a copy of copy." This would imply that the cure for insomnia involves bringing the real thing closer, as Plato's freed prisoner does when he journeys toward the sun. But the opening credit sequence suggests otherwise. The credits roll over a cinematic trip from deep within Edward Norton character's brain outward to his nasal passages and then onto his skin and back away from his face, at which point we discover that we have just traveled up what turns out to be a gun in his mouth (see Figure 6.10).[11] Though that excursion through the brain was of course computer-generated, the sweaty skin, those hair follicles, those pores the camera exposes – they consist of hundreds of extreme close-ups of Edward Norton's face. I take it that this opening sequence warns us that coming to understand the character Norton plays (which, in turn, will help us understand who Norton is on film) is not in fact a matter of looking very closely at him, but rather establishing the right distance from him, not too close, not too far. What exactly is this distance?

Like any really good movie, *Fight Club* proposes directions for thinking about the deep questions it poses. I will discuss two of its responses to the question of distance. First, there is the sequence in which the protagonist explains how a movie is put together. This sequence, which is aimed directly at us, occurs about a half hour into the film, right after Tyler proposes for the first time that the protagonist hit him and thus gives birth to the idea of "fight club." At this juncture, the protagonist as it were causes the frame to freeze and says in admiration that even a hummingbird couldn't catch Tyler at work.[12] Now, it may be true that

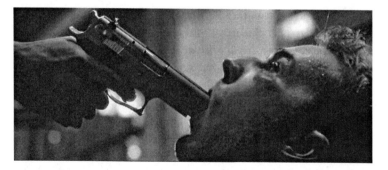

Figure 6.10 At what distance do we need to stand from the narrator to understand him?

the bird can't flap its wings as fast as a projector pixilates the frames of a film. But the hummingbird can't catch Tyler at work not because even it isn't fast enough but because it is incapable of understanding what Tyler is doing and why (see Figure 6.11). *We*, however, are in a position to worry about these matters, and this sequence is explicitly exhorting us to, as it were, take off our chains and look around more carefully. The exhortation comes in quite direct form: both the protagonist and Tyler are explicitly figured as film directors. The protagonist has stopped Fincher's film in order to speak directly to us, as he does, via voiceovers, throughout the film; the "cigarette burn" comes in exactly on Brad Pitt's cue; and Tyler of course helps himself to the director's task of deciding which available frames of film belong in what will be screened. So what do they want from us? *How* are we being asked to look at what we're seeing? Perhaps we should be looking for single, out-of-context frames spliced into this film. In fact, this search will be rewarded. As the narrator descends into madness at the beginning of the film, but before he frankly disassociates, Brad Pitt flits in and out of the frame in a split second several times, once, notably, when the protagonist, numbly working at a Xerox machine, talks about how his insomnia renders his representations of the world, as he puts it, à la Plato, copies of copies of copies.[13]

We are also treated, at the very end of the film, right before the credits role, to six or seven pornographic frames depicting a man's genitalia. What's important is that the penis we see for a quarter of a second or so is clearly something that is *not* important, not meant to work on us subconsciously: it's a joke that, at least after more than one viewing of the film, we are at least in principle in on. It's as though Fincher is suggesting that what ought to be disturbing when it comes to watching this film is not its pornographic dimension – its sex or violence – but rather what is right in front of our faces, what we look at but may not see.

I said that I would discuss a second way that *Fight Club* provides us with directions for establishing the right distance from which to fathom Edward Norton's character. Let me suggest that the film proposes that, in our current condition, at least, we as a culture cannot consider the question of the distance from which to understand others' existences in ungendered terms. For the protagonist's struggle with madness, with perpetual insomnia, is triggered by the depth of his feeling for Marla Singer, the woman whose palpable desperation at the support groups matches his own and threatens to expose him to, not least, himself. We can scarcely avoid reading the protagonist's conjuring up of Tyler as a massive flight from his panic in the face of his feeling for Marla, which, since it's his feeling, constitutes a flight from himself. Shortly after the protagonist stops going to support groups and casts his lot with Tyler, Marla takes an overdose of Xanax and phones the protagonist for help. But it is Tyler who comes to her rescue, Tyler who keeps her from falling fatally asleep by what can be described in literal terms as making violent love to her, and Tyler who, in his hyperbolic investment in a hyperbolic conception of masculinity, confirms her sense of her own worthlessness. The protagonist begins to see Tyler for who he is, begins to judge what's real, only when he is able to acknowledge his own, albeit unconscious part in Marla's degradation. His killing off of Tyler requires his acknowledging the Tyler in himself – his recognizing of the extent to which he both is and is not Tyler.

Figure 6.11 Tyler as director

At the end of the film, as Tyler's last and grandest plot comes to fruition and one corporate building after the next comes tumbling down, Edward Norton's character discovers where he has to stand in order to see the world clearly, which in his case means to acknowledge both his own and Marla's flesh-and-blood existence. The protagonist has just killed off Tyler, mythically by shooting himself, but, in reality, as it were, by gazing through a window – one precisely the size of a wide movie screen – at Marla as she is getting dragged off the bus by Tyler's thugs, and finding himself able to believe in his desire for her. ("And suddenly," he says, gun in his mouth, "I realize that all of this – the guns, the bombs, the revolution – has got something to do with a girl named Marla Singer.") Marla, who is absolutely furious, is hauled by the Space Monkeys to the protagonist's side and then stopped dead in her tracks when she sees the massive wound in his face.[14] Shocked and worried, she asks him what happened to him. He says that he's okay: "Marla, trust me. Everything's going to be fine." Right on (black-humor) cue, the bombs go off. As the buildings collapse in spectacular fashion, the protagonist takes Marla's hand and the two calmly, slowly, tentatively – as though on a first date – turn to watch the action together through the widescreen window. The right distance from which to bear witness to what's real, to judge the status of the world, *Fight Club* seems to claim at this moment, is not the one that would have you staring into the sun. Rather, it proposes – apropos of both Plato and Descartes, I claim – that the right distance is the one at which you are inclined to watch a movie with someone you love.

Notes

1 An earlier version of this essay was published as "Cogito Ergo Film: Plato, Descartes, and *Fight Club*," in *Film and Philosophy: Essays on Cinema after Wittgenstein and Cavell*, edited by Rupert Read and Jerry Goodenough (Florence, KY: Palgrave Macmillan, 2005).

2 Cavell's writings on film include *The World Viewed: Reflections on the Ontology of Film*, enlarged edition (Cambridge, MA: Harvard University Press, 1979; original edition 1971); *Pursuits of Happiness: The Hollywood Comedy of Remarriage* (Cambridge, MA: Harvard University Press, 1981); *Contesting Tears: The Melodrama of the Unknown Woman* (Chicago: University of Chicago Press, 1996); "On Makavejev on Bergman," "North by Northwest," "The Thought of Movies," "What Becomes of Things on Film?" and "Appendix: Film in the University," all from *Themes out of School: Effects and Causes* (New York: North

Point, 1984); "A Capra Moment," *Humanities* 6:4 (August 1985): 3–7; *Cities of Words: Pedagogical Letters on a Register of the Moral Life* (Cambridge, MA: Harvard University Press, 2004); "Psychoanalysis and Cinema" in *Images in our Souls: Cavell, Psychoanalysis, and Cinema*, edited by Joseph H. Smith and William Kerrigan (Baltimore: Johns Hopkins University Press, 1987); "Two Cheers for Romance," *Passionate Attachments: Thinking About Love*, edited by Willard Gaylin and Ethel Person (New York: Free Press, 1987); and "Who Disappoints Whom?" *Critical Inquiry* 15:3 (Spring 1989): 606–10.

3   This very same challenge is at the heart of *The Matrix*. Throughout that film, the protagonist, Neo, is desperate to know whether he is or is not "The One." No epistemic procedure – e.g., gathering evidence, consulting experts (The Oracle), steeling himself simply to believe and then act as though he's The One – gives him the answer he wants. The problem is resolved only when Neo acknowledges the feelings of love that he and Trinity share: this acknowledgment (which, à la a major theme of Cavell's writings, is not a function of what he does or can know) *transforms* Neo into The One, and, only then, leads to his belief in his status as The One.

4   The school of thinking I have in mind calls itself "cognitivist film theory." See, for example, Cynthia Freeland's argument in *The Naked and the Undead: Evil and the Appeal to Horror* (Boulder, CO: Westview Press, 1999). Freeland's view is that horror movies can be taken seriously by philosophers because they appeal to both our emotional and cognitive capacities – capacities Freeland understands to be essentially distinct. She writes, for example, "Horror films are designed to prompt emotions of fear, sympathy, revulsion, dread, anxiety, or disgust. And in doing so, they also stimulate thoughts about evil in its many varieties and degrees. . . . We may experience standard or predictable emotions (fear, revulsion, dread, relief), but then we also reflect on why and whether it is right to do so" (3; Freeland's emphasis). Other writings in cognitivist film theory include many of the essays in *Film Theory and Philosophy*, edited by Richard Allen and Murray Smith (Oxford: Oxford University Press, 1997) and *Passionate Views: Film, Cognition, and Emotion*, edited by Carl Plantinga and Greg M. Smith (Baltimore: Johns Hopkins University Press, 1999). See also Greg M. Smith, *Film Structure and the Emotion System* (New York: Cambridge University Press, 2003). Other prominent cognitivist film theorists include Noël Carroll and Gregory Currie.

5   Plato seems to succumb in his later dialogues – including the tenth book of the *Republic* – to the temptation of turning Socrates into a mouthpiece and the marketplace into a bully pulpit. But in the early dialogues Plato seems committed to the picture of philosophy I have sketched here. For speculation about why Plato became preachier in his later years, see the late work of Gregory Vlastos, especially chapters 2 and 3 of *Socrates, Ironist and Moral Philosopher* (Cambridge: Cambridge University Press and Ithaca, NY: Cornell University Press, 1991). For Cavell's most sustained discussion of the early Plato's vision of philosophy, see the introduction and chapter 1 of *Conditions Handsome and*

Unhandsome: The Constitution of Emersonian Perfectionism (Chicago: University of Chicago Press) and chapter 17 of *Cities of Words*, cited in note 1 above.

6 Laura Mulvey, "Visual Pleasure and Narrative Cinema," *Visual and Other Pleasures* (Bloomington, IN: Indiana University Press, 1989), 14–26. The essay was written in 1973 and originally published in 1975. It has been anthologized countless times and is arguably the most well-known essay in the history of academic film studies.

7 Of course, most professional philosophers are not completely thick, and so they would not deny that a film might be, in and of itself, an object of aesthetic interest. It's perfectly respectable within professional philosophy to worry about whether a film is really a work of art – about, that is, what a work of art is and whether some films, at least, meet the criteria. It's also permissible to engage in the cottage industry of talking about whether films work by appealing to our emotions or our cognition or both. (See note 4 above.) You can do what philosophers in general do and develop a top-down theory that *explains* what it is to be a film. What you can't do is suggest that films in and of themselves aspire to full participation in, and not just provocation of, philosophical conversation. You can't put any film, no matter how good it is, on an equal footing with the likes of an Aristotle or a Kant or a Quine.

8 More precisely, Descartes of course offers two arguments for the existence of God in the *Meditations*, a causal one in meditation three and an ontological one in meditation five.

9 Again, see Cavell's *Cities of Words*, chapter 17.

10 Though Norton's character is officially identified in the cast list of the film as "The Narrator," many commentators on the film refer to his character, whose real name is at best not made clear, as "Jack." This is because Norton's character, after reading a series of popular medical articles written from the whimsical point of view of various parts of the human body ("I am Jack's Medulla Oblongata," "I Am Jill's Nipple," and "I Am Jack's Colon"), starts to express his sense of his place in the world by riffs on the articles' titles: "I Am Jack's Cold Sweat," "I am Jack's Complete Lack of Surprise," "I Am Jack's Inflamed Sense of Rejection," "I Am Jack's Smirking Revenge," etc. Of course, to be Jack's X is not to be Jack. And, as I will explain momentarily, I think it's critical that the question of the narrator's identity is never resolved.

11 See *Fight Club*, 00:00:33 to 00:02:07.

12 See *Fight Club*, 00:32:10 to 00:33:33.

13 For this moment, see *Fight Club*, 00:03:57 to 00:04:10. For other moments in which Brad Pitt flashes into the frame for a split second, see *Fight Club*, 00:06:07 and 00:07:25.

14 See *Fight Club*, 02:15:13 to 02:16:10.

Chapter 7

Ben Caplan

NEVER BEEN KICKED*

TYLER:	Never been in a fight. You?
THE NARRATOR:	No, but that—that's a good thing.
TYLER:	No, it is not.[1]

1. Introduction

IN THIS PAPER, I ARGUE THAT Fight Club (1999) is a romantic comedy. More precisely, I argue that it is correct to perceive Fight Club in the genre romantic comedy. Let us call this conclusion "the romcom thesis." The romcom thesis leaves open two possibilities. The first possibility is that it is correct to perceive Fight Club both in the genre romantic comedy and in genres in which it is usually perceived: drama, say, or dark comedy.[2] The second possibility is that it is correct to perceive Fight Club both in the genre romantic comedy and in a hybrid genre – dark romantic comedy, say, or romantic dramedy, or even dark romantic dramedy – whose components include, not only the genre romantic comedy, but also genres in which it is usually perceived.[3] I am sympathetic to both of these possibilities, but I do not argue for either of them here.

Although the romcom thesis leaves these possibilities open, it is not trivial. For it is not also correct to perceive Fight Club in many other genres in which it is not usually perceived: documentary, say, or musical. And the romcom thesis bears on the evaluation of the film, since it turns out that, on this interpretation, Fight Club is rather clever. I return to Fight Club's cleverness in the penultimate section. I begin, in the next section, by presenting in some detail the theoretical framework that I rely on in the rest of the paper.

2. Categories and genres

2.1. Categories

In "Categories of Art," Kendall L. Walton (1970) argues for a pair of claims. The first claim is about the role that categories play in creating aesthetic appearances.

> *The category appearance claim*: which aesthetic properties a work of art appears to have depends on which category or categories that work of art is perceived in.[4]

Consider "Hush," which is roughly 44 minutes long and can be divided into three parts: the beginning, which is roughly 14 minutes long and has audible human dialogue; the middle, which is roughly 26 minutes long and has almost no audible human dialogue; and the end, which is roughly 4 minutes long and has audible human dialogue.[5] Perceived in the category *early 1920s silent film*, "Hush" appears to be alive with speech; whereas, perceived in the category *late 1990s television episode*, "Hush" appears to be eerily silent.

The second claim is about the role that categories play in creating aesthetic reality.

> *The category reality claim*: which aesthetic properties a work of art really has depends on which category or categories it is correct to perceive that work of art in. In particular, if a work of art W appears to have an aesthetic property F when W is perceived in a category C, and if it is correct to perceive W in C, then W really has F.[6]

In this case, "Hush" is an episode, one that was written and directed by Joss Whedon and that first aired in December 1999, from Season 4 of the television series *Buffy the Vampire Slayer* (1997–2003). So it is not correct to perceive it in the category *early 1920s silent film*, but it is correct to perceive it in the category *late 1990s television episode*. As a result, "Hush" really is eerily silent; but, even if it appears to be alive with speech when it is perceived in the category *early 1920s silent film*, it does not follow that it really is alive with speech.

2.2. Genres

The category appearance claim and the category reality claim are claims about categories in general. But each of these claims has an analogue that is about genres in particular.[7] First, the analogue of the category appearance claim is a claim about the role that genres play in creating aesthetic appearances.

> *The genre appearance claim*: which aesthetic properties a work of art appears to have depends on which genre or genres that work of art is perceived in.

To take a fictional example, consider *The New Surgeon at St. Oswald's*, a 1957 manuscript by Lavinia Armitage that Morag McCoo reads for a publisher in Charles Palliser's novel *Betrayals* (1995). Perceived in the genre *romance*, the ending – in which the new surgeon, Mr MacQuarrie ("Call me Jack"), eviscerates the naïve heroine, Nurse Marie Kelly – is surprising and out of place.[8] This is in fact how *The New Surgeon* is perceived in *Betrayals*: McCoo perceives the manuscript in the genre *romance* – her report begins "*Editorial department*: Romance" – and describes the ending as "wholly ina[p]propriate."[9] She suggests that "the final three or four sentences" be revised.[10] By contrast, perceived in the genre *horror*, the ending is satisfying and fitting. McCoo considers sending *The New Surgeon* to "the editor of our *Gothic Horror* list" but, for reasons that are not manifest, says that in that case "the author will have to be asked to substantially revise it."[11]

Second, the analogue of the category reality claim is a claim about the role that genres play in creating aesthetic reality.

> *The genre reality claim*: which aesthetic properties a work of art really has depends on which genre or genres it is correct to perceive that work of art in. In particular, if a work of art W appears to have an aesthetic property F when W is perceived in a genre G, and if it is correct to perceive W in G, then W really has F.

If it is correct to perceive *The New Surgeon* in the genre *romance*, then McCoo is right: the ending really is out of place and should be revised;

whereas, if it is correct to perceive the manuscript in the genre horror, then the ending really is fitting and does not need to be revised.

2.3. Four considerations

But how can we tell which category or genre it is correct to perceive a work of art in? For example, how can we tell which genre it is correct to perceive *The New Surgeon* in? Walton (1970: 212–13) mentions four considerations.[12] First, there is a consideration about the prevalence of a genre in a community.

> *The prevalence consideration*: if a genre G is "well established in and recognized by the society" in which a work of art W is produced, then that tells in favor of the claim that it is correct to perceive W in G.[13]

In *Betrayals*, we are not directly told anything about when the author, Armitage, was writing; but we are told that the reader, McCoo, was reading the manuscript in 1957, and – given McCoo's editorial department and the list whose editor she considers sending the manuscript to instead – *romance* and *horror* (or at least *Gothic horror*) were both recognized genres at the time. So, in this case, the prevalence consideration does not tell against the claim that it is correct to perceive *The New Surgeon* in the genre *romance* or the genre *horror*; but it does not tell in favor of the claim that it is correct to perceive that manuscript in one of those genres in particular.

Second, there is a consideration about the artist's intentions.

> *The intention consideration*: if the artist intends a work of art W to belong to a genre G or thinks of it as belonging to G, then that tells in favor of the claim that it is correct to perceive W in G.[14]

In *Betrayals*, we do not know what Armitage's intentions were. So the intention consideration does not tell in favor of, or against, the claim that it is correct to perceive *The New Surgeon* in any genre. And, in any case, it is easy to place too much importance on the intention consideration. It is not generally true that, if an artist intends a work of art to be a certain way or thinks of it as being that way, then that work of art really is that way. Walton (1970: 199) gives voice to this sentiment: "Surely (it seems) a Rembrandt portrait does not have (or lack) a sense of mystery in virtue of the fact that Rembrandt intended it to have (or lack) that quality, any

more than a contractor's intention to make a roof leakproof makes it so."[15]
For example, Richard Kelly, the writer and director of Donnie Darko (2001),
said that Frank (James Duval), Donnie Darko's (Jake Gyllenhaal's) sister's
boyfriend, has remembered what happened in a duplicate reality and is
trying to warn Donnie to flee the jet engine that is about to crush him
to death in his bed.[16] But Frank is just honking his horn as he drives away.
And M. Night Shyamalan, the writer and director of Signs (2002), said
that the film "doesn't have a twist" and added that, if you think that he
makes films with twists, "you're totally f—ked. It's just too complex."[17]
But Signs ends with the sudden revelation that everything that has been
making Rev. Graham Hess (Mel Gibson) lose his faith – especially the
death of his wife, Colleen (Patricia Kalember); the asthma of his son,
Morgan (Rory Culkin); and the compulsion of his daughter, Bo (Abigail
Breslin), to leave half-finished glasses of water lying around – is really
part of a divine plan. Examples like these suggest that we should not place
too much importance on artists' intentions in general or the intention
consideration in particular.

Third, there is a consideration about the features of the work of art itself.

> The features consideration: if a work of art W has "a relatively large number"
> of features that are standard with respect to a genre G and "a
> minimum" of features that are contra-standard with respect to G, then
> that tells in favor of the claim that it is correct to perceive W in G.[18]

A feature is standard with respect to a genre or category if and only if
"it is among those in virtue of which works in that [genre or] category
belong to that [genre or] category"; whereas a feature is contra-standard
with respect to a genre or category if and only if its "presence tends to
disqualify works as members of the [genre or] category."[19] (A feature that
is neither standard nor contra-standard with respect to a genre or category
is variable with respect to that genre or category.[20]) In the case of The New
Surgeon, that one of the main characters dies a gruesome death is standard
with respect to the genre horror but not with respect to the genre romance.
And that the manuscript ends with the evisceration of its protagonist is
contra-standard with respect to the genre romance but not with respect to
the genre horror. (To put it in a slogan, when it comes to genre body count
is a clue.) So the features consideration tells in favor of the claim that it
is correct to perceive The New Surgeon in the genre horror, and it tells against
the claim that it is correct to perceive the manuscript in the genre romance.

Fourth, there is a consideration about aesthetic evaluation.

The evaluation consideration: if a work of art W appears to be "better, or more interesting or pleasing aesthetically" when it is perceived in a genre G than it does when it is perceived in many other genres, then that tells in favor of the claim that it is correct to perceive W in G.[21]

I do not know how aesthetically pleasing a manuscript that ends with an evisceration appears to be when it is perceived in the genre *horror*; but, when it is perceived in the genre *romance*, a manuscript that ends with an evisceration appears to be less aesthetically pleasing than that.[22] So the evaluation consideration tells in favor of the claim that it is correct to perceive *The New Surgeon* in the genre *horror*, and it tells against the claim that it is correct to perceive the manuscript in the genre *romance*.

Care is required when using the evaluation consideration. As Walton (1970: 214) acknowledges, we cannot simply make up a genre G, point out that a work of art W appears to be aesthetically better when it is perceived in G than it does when it is perceived in many other genres, and conclude that it is correct to perceive W in G. Otherwise, we could make up the genre *film developed by two famous directors, one famous for being dark, the other famous for being sentimental, where the point is to confuse the audience about which director is responsible for which part.*[23] Let us call this genre *"dark and sentimental confusion."* We could then point out that *Artificial Intelligence: A.I.* (2001) appears to be aesthetically better when it is perceived in the genre *dark and sentimental confusion* than it does when it is perceived in the genre *drama* or the genre *science fiction*, say, and conclude that it is correct to perceive the film in the genre *dark and sentimental confusion.* But *Artificial Intelligence* is not good, and it is not correct to perceive it in that genre either. Still, neither the genre *horror* nor the genre *romance* is made up in the way that the genre *dark and sentimental confusion* is, since both the genre *romance* and the genre *horror* were recognized in the community in which *The New Surgeon* was read. So it is legitimate to use the evaluation consideration to support the conclusion that it is correct to perceive *The New Surgeon* in the genre *horror*.

In the rest of the paper, I discuss how Walton's four considerations – the prevalence consideration, the intention consideration, the features consideration, and the evaluation consideration – bear on the *romcom* thesis, the conclusion that it is correct to perceive *Fight Club* in the genre *romantic comedy*. Two of these considerations provide little or no support for the *romcom* thesis: the prevalence consideration does not tell against the thesis, but it does not tell in favor of it either (Section 3), and the intention consideration provides only a limited amount of support for the thesis (Section 4). By contrast, the features consideration and the evaluation consideration provide substantial support for the romcom thesis (Sections 5–8).

But, first, I discuss a complication in Walton's framework.

2.4. A complication

Walton (1970: 200) allows that one can simultaneously perceive a single work of art in multiple categories. To return to the example of "Hush," one can simultaneously perceive it in the categories *mass art* and *television episode*. Walton (1970: 216 n. 24) also allows that it can be correct to perceive a single work of art in multiple categories. For example, it might be correct to perceive "Hush" in the categories *mass art* and *television episode*. These claims are about categories in general, but they have analogues about genres in particular. So, for example, one can simultaneously perceive "Hush" in the genres *horror* and *teen drama*. And it might be correct to perceive "Hush" in both of those genres.

But now we face a problem. Suppose that, when it is perceived in the genre *horror*, "Hush" appears to have different properties than it appears to have when it is perceived in the genre *teen drama*. For example, suppose that the following claim is true.

(1) When it is perceived in the genre *horror*, "Hush" appears to be merely somewhat eerie; whereas, when it is perceived in the genre *teen drama*, it appears to be extremely eerie.

And suppose that it is correct to perceive "Hush" in both of those genres. That is, suppose that the following claim is true.

(2) It is correct to perceive "Hush" in both the genre *horror* and the genre *teen drama*.

The genre reality claim entails the following claim.

(3) If "Hush" appears to be merely somewhat eerie when it is perceived in the genre *horror*, and if it is correct to perceive "Hush" in the genre *horror*, then "Hush" really is merely somewhat eerie; and, if "Hush" appears to be extremely eerie when it is perceived in the genre *teen*

drama, and if it is correct to perceive "Hush" in the genre *teen drama*, then "Hush" really is extremely eerie.

Together, (1)–(3) entail the following claim.

(4) "Hush" is both merely somewhat eerie and also extremely eerie.

But (4) seems to be a contradiction.

It is not obvious what to do in the face of this apparent contradiction.[24] One might deny (1): that when it is perceived in the genre *horror*, "Hush" appears to be merely somewhat eerie; whereas, when it is perceived in the genre *teen drama*, it appears to be extremely eerie. But, even if this reply works in this case, I do not think that it will always work. I would be surprised if there were no cases in which a work of art appears to have apparently incompatible properties when it is perceived in different genres and in which it is plausible that it is correct to perceive that work of art in both of those genres.

Or one might deny (2): that it is correct to perceive "Hush" in both the genre *horror* and the genre *teen drama*. Instead, one might insist that it is correct to perceive "Hush" only in the hybrid genre *teen horror*.[25] But, again, even if this reply works in this case, I do not think that it will always work. First, I doubt that there will always be a coherent grand unified genre in which to perceive a work of art. It might be correct to perceive a work of art in both straight and ironic ways. But there might not be a coherent straight-and-ironic way of perceiving it. So, for example, it might be correct to perceive a film both as a satire and as something less comedic. But there might not be a coherent hybrid genre in which to perceive the film. And, second, I doubt that, even when there is a coherent grand unified genre in which to perceive a film, it will always be incorrect to perceive that film in any of the component genres. So, for example, I doubt that, whenever it is correct to perceive a film in the genre *romantic comedy*, it is always incorrect to perceive it in the genres *romance* and *comedy*. But I do not argue for either of those claims here.

Instead, I propose to deny (3): that if "Hush" appears to be merely somewhat eerie when it is perceived in the genre *horror*, and if it is correct to perceive "Hush" in the genre *horror*, then "Hush" really is merely somewhat eerie; and likewise for it appearing to be extremely eerie when it is perceived in the genre *teen drama*. This requires modifying the genre reality claim. I propose to replace the genre reality claim with the following claim.

The revised genre reality claim: which aesthetic properties a work of art really has depends on which genre or genres it is correct to perceive that work of art in. In particular, if a work of art W appears to have an aesthetic property F when W is perceived in a genre G, and if it is correct to perceive W in G, then there is a presumption in favor of W really having F; but this presumption can be defeated, especially if there are other genres in which it is correct to perceive W and if W appears to have different aesthetic properties when it is perceived in those genres.

(Parallel modifications to the category reality claim would also be called for.) This is not the only possible solution to the problem, but it is the solution that I adopt in the rest of this paper.

Walton (1970: 216 n. 24) concludes his discussion of the problem with an admonition: "None of these complications relieves the critic of the responsibility for determining in what way or ways it is correct to perceive a work." And so it is with *Fight Club*. What I argue is that it is correct to perceive *Fight Club* in the genre *romantic comedy*. Given the revised genre reality claim, this generates a presumption in favor of *Fight Club* having the aesthetic properties that it appears to have when it is perceived in the genre *romantic comedy*. But this presumption can be defeated.

I turn now to the case that can be made for the *romcom* thesis, the conclusion that it is correct to perceive *Fight Club* in the genre *romantic comedy*.

3. The prevalence consideration

The genre *romantic comedy* was well established and widely recognized in North America in 1999, when *Fight Club* was released. For example, *Never Been Kissed* – a romantic comedy in which Josie Geller (Drew Barrymore), a geeky copy editor at the *Chicago Sun-Times*, goes undercover as a high school student and falls for her hockey-playing English teacher, Sam Coulson (Michael Vartan) – was also released that year. So the prevalence consideration does not tell against the *romcom* thesis. But, of course, *romantic comedy* is not the only genre that was well established and widely recognized in North America in 1999. For example, the genre *mockumentary* was, too: *Best in Show*, a mockumentary about the obsessive owners of show dogs, was released in 2000. So the prevalence consideration does not tell against the claim that it is correct to perceive Fight Club in the genre mockumentary either, and hence it does not tell in favor of the claim that it is correct to perceive that film in either of those genres in particular. So, if we are looking for support for the romcom thesis, we should look to other considerations.

4. The intention consideration

Those behind Fight Club thought of it as belonging to the genre dark comedy. David Fincher, the director, compared it to the dark comedy Dr. Strangelove or: How I Stopped Worrying and Learned to Love the Bomb (1964), described it as "absurdist," and said, "It's a pitch-black comedy."[26] Jim Uhls, the screenwriter, said that "there was nothing so dark" in the film that "it couldn't be funny."[27] Chuck Palahniuk, the author of the novel that the film was based on, said that the film is a comedy – at least until Tyler Durden (Brad Pitt) burns the narrator's (Edward Norton's) hand with lye.[28] Edward Norton also compared the film to Dr. Strangelove, described it as "a comedy, or a black comedy, with a heavy element of satire," and said, "It's a comedy. It's a dark comedy."[29] Helena Bonham Carter, who played Marla Singer, said that the film is "satirical" and "intensely funny in a dark way."[30] Brad Pitt compared the film to the satire A Clockwork Orange (1971) and said, "I got into such an argument with a journalist. I tried to tell him this is a comedy. I got nowhere with him."[31]

A lot of the film is supposed to be funny: for example, Marla and the narrator being the only white people at a support group for people with sickle cell anemia (Fincher: "This was a joke that was often lost on preview audiences")[32]; the narrator punching Tyler for the first time (Fincher: "I remember just almost falling out of my chair it was so funny. . . . It just cracked me up")[33]; a bag of human fat stolen from a liposuction clinic tearing on a fence topped with barbed wire (Bonham Carter: "This is such a disgusting but horribly darkly comic scene")[34]; the narrator beating himself up in his boss's (Zach Grenier's) office (Fincher: "Jerry Lewis is not dead")[35]; three cops – Detectives Andrew (Van Quattro), Kevin (Markus Redmond), and Walker (Michael Girardin) – trying to castrate the narrator (Pitt: "I think it's so funny")[36]; and the narrator talking in a "f—ked up" voice after having shot his bottom left molar out the side of his face (Fincher: "People just started cracking up. And that's hopefully what they should be doing. That's my feeling about what they should be doing").[37]

Figure 7.1 Marla hugging the narrator

At least one person behind Fight Club thought of it as belonging to the genre *romantic comedy*. Uhls described the film as "a romantic comedy, but not a typical romantic comedy."[38] Given the intention consideration, that Uhls thought of Fight Club as a romantic comedy provides some support for the *romcom* thesis. But it is not clear whether Fincher, Palahniuk, Norton, Bonham Carter, or Pitt thought of the film as a romantic comedy, although Fincher described Marla as a "romantic nihilist"; Norton said – probably facetiously – that in a scene in which the narrator apologizes to Marla the narrator "was so romantic" until she said, "You're spectacular in bed"; and Palahniuk talked about the film's "romantic ending."[39] And, in any case, as I suggested in Section 2, there is reason not to place too much importance on the intention consideration. So, if we are looking for more than minimal support for the *romcom* thesis, we should continue looking to further considerations.

5. The features consideration I: plot

It is probably impossible to provide informative necessary and sufficient conditions for being in most genres.[40] I do not think that the genre *romantic comedy* is an exception. Still, many genres have standard plots. The following four plot elements are all standard for the genre *romantic comedy*: (i) mismatched romantic leads meet under unusual circumstances; (ii) someone is mistaken about someone's identity; (iii) one of them comes to a sudden realization; and (iv) they end up together. Fight Club has all of those plot elements. Given the features consideration, this tells substantially in favor of the *romcom* thesis.

5.1. Meet-cute

In some romantic comedies, the romantic leads do not meet early on. For example, in *Sleepless in Seattle* (1993), although Annie Reed (Meg Ryan), a Baltimore journalist, has heard Sam Baldwin (Tom Hanks), a Seattle architect, on Dr. Marcia Fieldstone's (Caroline Aaron's) radio show and he has glimpsed her standing across the road, they do not actually meet until the end of the film. But, in most romantic comedies, the romantic leads, who are often mismatched, meet early on, often under unusual circumstances.[41] This is a standard feature of the genre *romantic comedy*. It is sometimes called a "meet-cute." "Say a man and a woman both need something to sleep in, and they both go to the same men's pajama department. And the man says to the salesman, 'I just need bottoms'. And the woman says, 'I just need a top'. They look at each other, and that's the meet-cute," an old-time screenwriter, Arthur Abbot (Eli Wallach), explains in *The Holiday* (2006).[42] For example, early on in *Roman Holiday* (1953), an American journalist in Rome, Joe Bradley (Gregory Peck), who is walking home from a late-night poker game meets the princess of an unnamed European country, Ann (Audrey Hepburn), who is "snoozing away on a public street," sleeping off a sedative after having escaped from her country's embassy. And, early on in *Love Actually* (2003), a bashful young man, John (Martin Freeman), meets a friendly young woman, Just Judy (Joanna Page), when they are stand-ins for a copulating couple on the set of a pornographic film.

Fight Club is no different. Marla and the narrator are mismatched, and they meet under unusual circumstances. He is an uptight boy who wears button-down oxford shirts, lives in a condo, and works for a major car company. She is a reckless girl who wears black, lives in a seedy hotel, and sells clothes she steals from laundromats. They meet in a support group for people with a disease that neither of them has. He is there for the catharsis that allows him to sleep. She is there for the free coffee.

5.2. Mistaken identity

In some romantic comedies, no one is mistaken about who or what anyone is. For example, in *Four Weddings and a Funeral* (1994), Carrie (Andie McDowell) is not an American con artist who pretends to be a British noblewoman, and Charles (Hugh Grant) is not a paleontologist who pretends to be a big-game hunter. But, in many romantic comedies, the romantic leads are mistaken about who or what someone is. This is also a standard feature of the genre *romantic comedy*. In a normal case of mistaken identity, one of the romantic leads is mistaken about who or what someone else is. For example, in *Charade* (1963), Brian Cruikshank (Cary Grant), a Treasury Department official at the US embassy in Paris, pretends in succession to be Peter Joshua, a charming divorced man; Alexander Dyle, a man who is trying to solve the murder of his brother, a wartime associate of Regina Lampert's (Audrey Hepburn's) late husband; and Adam Canfield, a thief who is after a quarter of a million dollars. Brian knows that he is not a charming divorced man, or Regina's late husband's wartime associate's brother, or a thief. But Regina does not. Complications ensue. (At one point, Regina says to Brian, "Do you realize you've had three names in the past two days? I don't even know who I'm talking to anymore.")[43] And, in *Down with Love* (2003), Catcher Block (Ewan McGregor) – star journalist at *KNOW*, the magazine for men in the know, and "ladies' man, man's man, and man about town" – pretends to be a shy US astronaut, Major Zip Martin, to write an exposé on a "cool blonde," Barbara Novack, "a girl from Maine who wrote a book and came to New York," who is really a "bashful brunette," Nancy Brown (Renée Zellweger), who used to be his secretary. Catcher thinks that he has fooled her into thinking that he is an astronaut. But he has not; she knows that he is really her former boss. What he does not know is that she is really his former secretary. Again, complications ensue. (In a fantastic three-and-a-half-minute monologue, Nancy sums up the plot so far. "I knew that . . . you would have to go undercover, assume a false identity, and pretend to be the kind of man who would make the kind of girl I was pretending to be fall in love," she explains.)[44]

In an inverted case of mistaken identity, by contrast, one of the romantic leads is mistaken about who or what they are. This is what happens in *Fight Club*. The narrator thinks that he has a better-looking roommate, who he is jealous of, who is having sex with Marla, but he does not; he is the one who is having sex with her. The narrator does not know that he does not have a roommate, but Marla does. And, yes, complications ensue.

This is an innovative use of mistaken identity in a romantic comedy. Indeed, it is *Fight Club*'s key variation on the genre. As far as I know, *Fight Club* is the only romantic comedy that features an inverted case of mistaken identity that does not rely on amnesia and in which the audience does not know what a character does not know. In this respect, *Fight Club* is, as Uhls says, not a typical romantic comedy. There are other films that feature inverted cases of mistaken identity. For example, in *Overboard* (1987), a rich socialite, Joanna Stayton (Goldie Hawn), falls off her husband's yacht and is misled into believing that she is Annie Proffitt, the wife of a lowly carpenter, Dean Proffitt (Kurt Russell). And, in *Angel Heart* (1987), a seedy detective, Harold Angel (Mickey Rourke), is hired to find a missing bandleader, Johnny Favourite. What Harold does not know is that, to avoid giving his soul to the devil as promised, Johnny the bandleader became Harold the detective. But both of these films rely on amnesia. And neither of them is a romantic comedy in which the audience does not know what a character does not know. In *Angel Heart*, the audience does not know what Harold does not know, but the film is not a romantic comedy; it is a horror or mystery film. And *Overboard* is a romantic comedy, but the audience knows that the woman who thinks that she is a carpenter's wife is the socialite who fell off her husband's yacht. As we will see in Section 8, *Fight Club*'s key variation on the genre *romantic comedy* matters to the evaluation of the film.[45]

5.3. Sudden realization

Some romantic comedies come to a climax when someone who is not one of the romantic leads realizes something about someone who is one of the romantic leads. For example, *The Incredibly True Adventure of Two Girls in Love* (1995) comes to a climax when Evelyn Roy (Stephanie Berry) finds her daughter, Evie (Nicole Ari Parker), a black girl who loves opera and whose father gave her a Range Rover, in bed with Randy Dean (Laurel Holloman), a white girl who digs classic rock and who works at a garage, and when Randy's aunt Rebecca (Kate Stafford) finds out that Randy does not have enough credits to graduate from high school.[46] But most romantic comedies come to a climax when one of the romantic leads realizes something about another romantic lead: when one of the romantic leads realizes how they feel about or that they really want to be with another romantic lead, say. This is also a standard feature of the genre *romantic comedy*. For example, *Notting Hill* (1999) comes to a climax when a British bookseller, William Thacker (Hugh Grant), realizes that he has been a "daft prick" for turning down an American movie star, Anna Scott (Julia Roberts), and rushes to her press conference. And *Keeping the Faith* (2000) comes to a climax when Father Brian Finn (Edward Norton) makes Rabbi Jake Schram (Ben Stiller) realize that he should not be standing around when a high-powered shiksa businesswoman who is their childhood friend, Anna Riley (Jenna Elfman), is about to leave forever ("It's a very simple situation: you're in love with her, she's in love with you, and she is leaving in about two hours," Finn tells him).[47]

Fight Club is a little, but not much, different. The film comes to a climax when the narrator realizes that he does not have a better-looking roommate and that he likes Marla after all. "I've come to realize something very, very important," he tells her. "The full extent of our relationship wasn't really clear to me up until now," he says. "What I've come to realize is that I really like you, Marla," he says. (Fincher said that this scene was rewritten and reshot so that the narrator was less "coy" and more forceful.[48]) What is unusual in this case is that the narrator tries to send Marla away, but he is doing that to protect her from him and from the bad things that he knows are about to happen.

5.4. Happy ending

A few romantic comedies do not end with the romantic leads ending up together. For example, Ann and Joe do not end up together in Roman Holiday. She resumes her royal duties, and he leaves her final press conference in Rome alone. (Still, in a scene that is echoed in Notting Hill, she says at that press conference that she enjoyed her visit to Rome most of all.) But almost all romantic comedies end with the romantic leads ending up together. This is also a standard feature of the genre romantic comedy, what James Harvey (1998: 313) calls "the conventional windup bringing hero and heroine together." But what the romantic leads do when they end up together is a variable feature of the genre. Usually, they kiss. For example, Four Weddings and a Funeral ends with Carrie and Charles embracing passionately in a thunderstorm. But sometimes they do something a little more demure. For example, Sleepless in Seattle ends with Annie and Sam holding hands in an elevator at the top of the Empire State Building as the doors close in front of them. And Notting Hill ends with Anna – who is now pregnant – and William on a park bench, their fingers intertwined, she gazing off into the distance and resting her head on his lap, he reading Captain Corelli's Mandolin.

Fight Club is no different. The film ends with Marla and the narrator holding hands and looking at each other as buildings implode in front of them. "Trust me. Everything's going to be fine. You met me at a very strange time in my life," he says. This is, I think, a straightforwardly happy ending. Palahniuk disagrees. He thinks that the only happy ending is death.[49] But, if so, then tragedies like Baz Luhrmann's *Romeo + Juliet* (1996) would have happy endings, whereas comedies like Trevor Nunn's *Twelfth Night: Or What You Will* (1996) would have unhappy endings, in which case *Fight Club* not having a happy ending would be consistent with the romcom thesis.

Palahniuk points out that the "romantic ending" is "truncate[d]" by an intercut image of a penis.[50] But that does not mean that the ending is not really romantic. The intercut image of a penis is a self-referential gag, like showing a changeover dot in the upper right-hand corner of the screen in a scene in which Tyler points to that part of the screen and explains what a changeover dot is ("In the industry, we call them 'cigarette burns'"); showing sprockets in a scene in which Tyler says, "We are the all-singing, all-dancing crap of the world" and again in a flashback to that scene in which the narrator says the line; the narrator's talking about changeovers when he has just realized that he does not have a better-looking roommate ("It's called a 'changeover'. The movie goes on, and nobody in the audience has any idea"); or Tyler mentioning "flashback humor" in a scene at the end of the film that continues the flashback that the film begins with. Sometimes these gags are clues to what is not really real: there is no guy who is about to become the narrator's better-looking roommate and who explains what a changeover dot is, and the narrator does not have a better-looking roommate who says, "We are the all-singing, all-dancing crap of the world." But sometimes they are merely gags: the narrator really does say, "We are the all-singing, all-dancing crap of the world," he really does realize that he does not have a better-looking roommate, and the scene at the end of the film really does continue a flashback that the film begins with. The intercut image of a penis is, I think, merely one of those gags. (Uhls had originally intended the image of a penis to be intercut, from the narrator's point of view, in a scene in which his boss is talking.[51])

Palahniuk also points out that the narrator still has to deal with his acolytes, the Space Monkeys (each of whom is "like a monkey ready to be shot into space, a space monkey ready to sacrifice himself for the greater good"), who are determined to carry out their destructive missions, even in the face of the narrator's explicit orders to stop. This, I think, is one of the two biggest problems for the romcom thesis.

(The other problem, which I discuss below in Section 7, is the violence.) But maybe the acolytes are not such a problem. Maybe, once the buildings have been blown up, they do not have further havoc to wreak. Maybe how to deal with the acolytes is merely one of those details that is not explicitly resolved in the film but will get resolved somehow, like how Annie and Sam will decide whether to live in Baltimore or in Seattle in *Sleepless in Seattle* or how Evie and Randy will deal with Evie's irate mother and Randy's irate aunt in *The Incredibly True Adventure of Two Girls in Love*.

One might also think that, because the narrator is psychotic and Marla is suicidal, they are doomed. Although they might not seem well suited, Uhls said that their relationship "in fact does work for them."[52] In many romantic comedies the romantic leads are well suited in the film, even if people like them would be ill suited in real life. This might be a standard feature of the genre *romantic comedy*. For example, an American movie star with a bit of a temper and a British bookseller with a bit of a stammer are well suited in *Notting Hill*, even if in real life they would not be. Richard Curtis, the writer, described the film as "a concealed fairy tale—the Princess & the Woodcutter as it were."[53] He said that, "by the end of writing the film, I think I'd started to believe it myself, that it was absolutely possible for just some guy to stay cool in the face of a huge star, and for things to work out."[54] He eventually came to his senses, though. "But don't be taken in," he said.[55] Really, it is all a "big lie."[56] And Sally Albright (Meg Ryan), who is "cheerful and chirpy and relentlessly, pointlessly, unrealistically, idiotically optimistic" ("Basically, I'm a happy person. And I don't see that there's anything wrong with that") and Harry Burns (Billy Crystal), who is "the prince of darkness, the master of the worst-case scenario," "bleak and depressed" ("When I buy a new book, I always read the last page first. That way, in case I die before I finish, I know how it ends"), get together after years of being friends and are well suited in *When Harry Met Sally . . .* (1989).[57] But Nora Ephron, the writer, pointed out that in real life people do not usually get together after years of being friends or, if they do, their relationship probably will not last. "If you wanted to be honest about it, these things usually don't happen that way. . . . It's probably not going to work," she said.[58] And Carrie Fisher, who played one of Sally's friends, pointed out that in real life people like Sally and Harry are not well suited for each other. "They seem to be suited. But, really, in terms of statistics? Divorce," she said.[59]

6. The features consideration II: mood or tone

When it comes to standard features, I am mainly interested in plot. But there is more to genre than plot. As Noel Carroll (1982: 104) notes in criticizing Stanley Cavell's (1981) plot-based account of the genre *Hollywood comedy of remarriage*, "Genres seem to share more than plots; they share characters, moods, settings, tempos, scenes, tones, possibly themes or allegorical subject matter, perhaps actors and their associated qualities, etc." I cannot here do justice to all of the rich texture of the genre *romantic comedy*.[60] But there is a mood or tone that is standard for the genre and that is often evidenced in antagonistic but witty banter. *Fight Club* shares the antagonistic but witty banter and this mood or tone. Given the features consideration, this also tells substantially in favor of the *romcom* thesis.

In some romantic comedies, the romantic leads get along just fine. For example, in *Notting Hill*, although Anna has a bit of a temper, she and William "get on very well," in the words of his Welsh roommate Spike (Rhys Ifans). (Spike mentions this as evidence that William has a "nice opportunity to . . . slip her one.") But, in many romantic comedies, there is a certain friction or antagonism between the romantic leads, at least until they realize that they are really made for each other. This is a standard feature of the genre *romantic comedy*. For example, in *When Harry Met Sally . . .*, Harry explains to Sally why he never takes anyone to the airport at the beginning of a relationship.

> HARRY: Because eventually things move on and you don't take someone to the airport, and I never wanted anyone to say to me, "How come you never take me to the airport anymore?"
>
> SALLY: It's amazing. You look like a normal person but actually you are the Angel of Death.

Years later, when Sally sees Harry in a bookstore, she describes him to her friend Marie (Carrie Fisher) as "obnoxious."

> MARIE: This is just like in the movies. Remember in *The Lady Vanishes* when she says to him, "You are the most obnoxious man I have ever met"—
>
> SALLY (CORRECTING HER): "The most contemptible."
>
> MARIE (CONTINUING): —and they fall madly in love.[61]

And, in *You've Got Mail* (1998), when one of the owners of the chain that has just opened up a megastore near a small bookstore on the Upper West Side that it will soon put out of business, Joe Fox (Tom Hanks), shows up for a date with someone he met online, he realizes that his date is with Kathleen Kelly (Meg Ryan), the woman he is about to put out of business. She complains that, when they first met in her bookstore, he did not tell her that he was her competition.

KATHLEEN: You lied to me.
JOE: I didn't lie to you.
KATHLEEN: You did too.
JOE: No, I didn't.
KATHLEEN: Yes, you did.
JOE: I did not.
KATHLEEN: You did too.
JOE: I did not.
KATHLEEN: You did too.
JOE: I did not.
KATHLEEN: Yeah, you did too.

She goes on to tell him that his store is a "theme park, multi-level, homogenized mochaccino-land." "You've deluded yourself into thinking that you're some sort of benefactor. But no one will ever remember you, Joe," she says. "You are nothing but a suit."

Fight Club is no different. Marla and the narrator express disdain for each other. "If I did have a tumor, I'd call it 'Marla'," he tells us in a voiceover near the beginning of the film. "You're intolerable," she tells him near the end of the film. And, in between, they engage in antagonistic but witty banter. When they first speak, the narrator, who goes by different names at different support groups, confronts her.

THE NARRATOR: I've seen you. I saw you at melanoma. I saw you at tuberculosis. I saw you at testicular cancer.
MARLA: I saw you practicing this.
THE NARRATOR: Practicing what?
MARLA: Telling me off. Is it going as well as you hoped, Rupert?

After they work out who gets to go to which support group, she takes her leave.

MARLA: Looks like this is goodbye.

THE NARRATOR: Well, let's not make a big thing out of it, okay?

MARLA: How's this for not making a big thing? (*She walks out.*)

Weeks later, she calls him.

THE NARRATOR: I'm just on my way out.

MARLA: Me, too. I've got a stomach full of Xanax.

THE NARRATOR: So you're staying in tonight, then?

Later, at his place, she approaches him wearing a dress.

MARLA: It's a bridesmaid's dress. Someone loved it intensely for one day then tossed it . . . like a sex-crime victim, underwear inside out, bound with electrical tape.

THE NARRATOR: Well, then, it suits you.

MARLA: You can borrow it sometime.

Later still, she asks him to come over to her place to give her a breast exam. She thanks him when he has finished.

MARLA: I wish I could return the favor.

THE NARRATOR: There's not a lot of breast cancer in the men in my family.

MARLA: Could check your prostate.

When she kisses him on the side of the mouth, he asks, "Are we done?"

According to Harvey (1998: 107), it is this "combination of love and toughness" that was new in the films that define the genre *romantic comedy* as it emerged in Hollywood in 1934. These films, including *It Happened One Night* (1934), feature a "new kind of energy," something "slangy, combative, humorous, unsentimental—and powerfully romantic."[62] The energy between Marla and the narrator is, I think, slangy, combative, humorous, and unsentimental in this way.

Figure 7.2 The narrator's fantasy recollection

7. The features consideration III: contra-standard features

There is a lot of male-on-male pugilism and urban terrorism in Fight Club. This sort of thing does not usually happen in romantic comedies. For example, in Sleepless in Seattle, Sam does not pummel his brother-in-law, Greg (Victor Garber), to bits, and Annie and Sam do not watch the Empire State Building collapse. Pugilism and terrorism are contra-standard relative to the genre romantic comedy. Granted, there are a few other romantic comedies with violence in them. For example, in Punch-Drunk Love (2002), Barry Egan (Adam Sandler) brawls with thugs from a phone sex line. And, in Mr. and Mrs. Smith (2005), John and Jane Smith (Brad Pitt and Angelina Jolie) try to kill each other. But these films are exceptional, and if it is correct to perceive them in the genre romantic comedy it is despite the violence in them. Ordinarily, it would not be correct to perceive a film with as much pugilism and terrorism as Fight Club in the genre romantic comedy. So what is it about Fight Club in virtue of which it is correct to perceive it in the genre romantic comedy despite the contra-standard pugilism and terrorism?

In Fight Club, the terrorism is really about something more familiar in romantic comedies: a girl. Or so the narrator tells us at the beginning of the film. "And, suddenly, I realize that all of this – the gun, the bombs, the revolution – has got something to do with a girl named 'Marla Singer'," he says. It is difficult to say what, exactly, the pugilism of Fight Club or the terrorism of Project Mayhem has to do with Marla Singer.

But here is a hypothesis. The narrator created a macho persona because he thinks adopting that persona will help him get Marla. Unfortunately, the macho persona that he created is insane; and, as a result, people get beaten up and things get blown up. The timing fits. It is only after he meets Marla that the narrator thinks that he meets a soap salesman by the name of 'Tyler Durden' on a plane. (We see images of Pitt for one frame before the narrator meets Marla. But, except for the flashback that the film opens with, the first time that Pitt appears on screen for more than one frame is when we see him in an airport as the narrator passes by. This is just after the narrator has talked to Marla for the first time.) Tyler suggests that the narrator created a macho persona because he thought that adopting that persona would make him seem more attractive. "All the ways you wish you could be, that's me. I look like you wanna look, I f—k like you wanna f—k. I am smart, capable, and, most importantly, I am free in all the ways that you are not," he says to the narrator. Fincher suggested that the narrator created a macho persona to deal with Marla. He said that, in the "subliminal Brads," Tyler looks like he is telling the narrator, "I can solve a lot of these problems for you."[63] One of these problems is probably Marla, since the last time a single-frame image of Pitt appears is when Marla, who the narrator has yet to talk to, is walking away from a support group. And Bonham Carter said that the narrator created a macho persona to deal with, and be with, Marla. She said, "I think Marla—definitely if it was not for Marla, Tyler would not be engendered and that the need to invent Tyler comes from meeting Marla; or, in confronting Marla, somebody who he could possibly have a relationship with, he's too scared and retreats and invents this character that he feels could have a relationship rather than himself."[64] And this macho persona is insane. Fincher described Tyler as the "insane, you know, hyper-stylized masculine side" of the narrator.[65] Adopting a hyper-stylized masculine persona might be a good way to get Marla. Adopting an insanely masculine persona is a good way to beat people up and blow things up. If this hypothesis is correct, then Fight Club and Project Mayhem are merely byproducts of the narrator's attempt to get the girl.

8. The evaluation consideration

When *Fight Club* is perceived in the genre *romantic comedy*, the film appears to have an aesthetic vice: the second half of the film appears somewhat slow, since it is focused on pugilism and terrorism, which are at best byproducts of the narrator's attempt to get Marla. But, when it is perceived in the genre *romantic comedy*, Fight Club appears to have an aesthetic virtue: the film appears to be clever in a way that exploits its key variation on the genre. *Fight Club* does not appear to be clever in this way when it is perceived in the genre *drama* or *dark comedy*. Given the evaluation consideration, this tells in favor of the *romcom* thesis.

Fight Club's key variation on the genre, recall, is that it features an inverted case of mistaken identity that does not rely on amnesia and in which the audience does not know what a character does not know. It is this variation that allows the film to fool the audience about just what kind of romantic comedy it is watching. And, for those of us who like to be fooled fairly, that is aesthetically a good thing.[66]

Almost all romantic comedies end with the romantic leads ending up together after having overcome some obstacles. Ephron has distinguished two kinds of romantic comedy.[67] In a gentile romantic comedy, the main obstacle is "external": there is a third party, say.[68] For example, in *Sleepless in Seattle*, one of the main obstacles to Annie and Sam ending up together – other than the fact that she lives in Baltimore, he lives in Seattle, and they have never met – is that Annie is engaged to Walter (Bill Pullman) and that Sam is dating Victoria (Barbara Garrick). And, in *Four Weddings and a Funeral*, one of the main obstacles to Carrie and Charles ending up together is that she is engaged and then married to an older Scottish politician, Hamish (Corin Redgrave) and that he is engaged to an ex-girlfriend, Henrietta (Anna Chancellor). In a Jewish romantic comedy, by contrast, the main obstacle is "internal": one of the parties – typically a guy – is neurotic, say.[69] Just about every Woody Allen film is an example of this. And, although Sally and Harry are occasionally married to or dating other people in *When Harry Met Sally . . .*, Rob Reiner, the director, said that the main obstacle to their ending up together is their own shtick, their own "*Sturm und Drang*."[70]

In *Fight Club*, it seems that Tyler is the main obstacle to Marla and the narrator ending up together. But it turns out that Tyler *is* the narrator. So what at first appears to be an external obstacle – a third party – turns out to be an internal obstacle: a psychosis of one of the parties. Along these lines, Uhls thought of *Fight Club* as a romantic comedy that is about something internal to the characters: their psychologies. After saying that the film is a romantic comedy, Uhls said,

It has to do with the characters' attitudes toward a healthy relationship, which is a lot of behavior which *seems* unhealthy and harsh to each other, but in fact does work for them—because both characters are out on the edge psychologically.[71]

(Fincher described their relationship a little more bluntly: "She's trying to make this work, and this guy is so nuts."[72]) When it is perceived in the genre *romantic comedy*, *Fight Club* at first appears to be a gentile romantic comedy but turns out to be a Jewish romantic comedy instead. That is rather clever.

Perceiving *Fight Club* in the genre *romantic comedy* is not like perceiving *Artificial Intelligence* in the genre *dark and sentimental confusion*. For *romantic comedy* is an established genre (see Section 3) and Uhls at least thought of *Fight Club* as belonging to that genre (see Section 4). *Artificial Intelligence* might appear to be good when it is perceived in the genre *dark and sentimental confusion* in ways that it does not when it is perceived in many other genres, but that does not tell in favor of the claim that it is correct to perceive it in that genre. By contrast, there is no such reason to think that *Fight Club* appearing to be clever when it is perceived in the genre *romantic comedy* in a way in which it does not when it is perceived in many other genres does not tell in favor of the claim that it is correct to perceive it is in the genre *romantic comedy*.

9. Conclusion

The screenwriter of *Fight Club* thought of the film as belonging to the genre *romantic comedy*. The film contains several plot elements that are standard, and has a mood or tone that is standard, for the genre *romantic comedy*. And, when it is perceived in the genre *romantic comedy*, the film appears to be clever in a way that it does not when it is perceived in many other genres. Following Walton, these considerations all tell in favor of the *romcom* thesis. The romcom thesis puts us in a better position to figure out which aesthetic properties the film really does have. In particular, since the film appears to be a bit boring in the second half when it is perceived in the genre *romantic comedy*, and since it is correct to perceive the film in that genre, the revised genre thesis entails that there is a presumption in favor of the claim that the film really is a bit boring in the second half. This presumption might be defeated, though, if it is correct to perceive

Fight Club in other genres and if the film appears to be less boring in the second half when it is perceived in those genres. More importantly, since *Fight Club* appears to be rather clever when it is perceived in the genre *romantic comedy*, and since it is correct to perceive the film in that genre, the revised genre thesis entails that there is a presumption in favor of the claim that the film really is rather clever. In principle, this presumption could be defeated if it is correct to perceive *Fight Club* in other genres and if it appears to be less clever when it is perceived in those genres. But I like to think that, even in that case, the presumption would not be defeated.

Notes

*   For comments and discussion, thanks to Eva Della Lana, Joyce Jenkins, Carl Matheson, Rob Shaver, Brian Walter, and Thomas Wartenberg.
1   Edward Norton's character is called "Jack" in the script. See www.dailyscript. com/scripts/fightclub_2_98.html (accessed 12 June 2009). But the character is called "The narrator" in the closing credits. In the text, I follow the closing credits.
2   Metacritic lists the genre of *Fight Club* as "drama." See www.metacritic. com/video/titles/fightclub (accessed 3 June 2009). The Internet Movie Database lists the genre of *Fight Club* as "Action/Crime/Drama/Thriller" and includes "Dark Comedy," "Social Satire," "Satire," and "Dark Humor" among the approximately 175 plot keywords for the movie. (But then that list also includes "Reality," "Penguin," "Donut," and "Reference to Martha Stewart.") Neither "Romance" nor "Romantic Comedy" is on the list of plot keywords. "Love Hate Relationship" is, but it is not clear whether the love–hate relationship in question is between the narrator and Marla Singer or rather between the narrator and Tyler Durden. See www.imdb.com/ title/tt0137523/ and www.imdb.com/title/tt0137523/keywords (accessed 3 June 2009).
3   *Dramedy* is a hybrid genre whose components are the genres *comedy* and *drama*. Of course, *romantic comedy* is itself a hybrid genre. But that does not prevent it from being a component of other hybrid genres.
4   See Walton 1970: 201–10. Strictly speaking, Walton's (1970: 201) claim is that "what aesthetic properties a work seems to have . . . depends (in part) on which of its features are standard, which variable, and which contra-standard for us." But which features of a work are standard, which variable, and which contra-standard for us depends on which categories we perceive that work in. See Walton 1970: 201. Standard, variable, and contra-standard features are discussed below in the text.
5   The beginning part begins at the beginning and ends at the end of Act I. So it includes the opening credits and a wordless scene in which people's voices

are stolen. The middle part begins at the beginning of Act II and ends late in Act IV. So it includes scenes in which a computerized elevator voice intones 47 words, a newscaster on TV reads 154 words, a character uses a Stephen Hawking-style voice synthesizer to produce 34 words, and a character screams audibly but wordlessly. The end part begins late in Act IV and ends at the end. So it includes the closing credits. A version of the script is available here: www.buffyworld.com/buffy/scripts/066_scri.html (accessed 3 June 2009).

6 See Walton 1970: 210–16.

7 It is not clear whether Walton thinks of genres as categories. In the version of the paper that appeared in the *Philosophical Review* in 1970, he says that perceptually distinguishable categories "include media, genre, styles, forms and so forth"; whereas, in the version of the paper that is reprinted in Walton 2008, he writes of perceptually distinguishable categories and "other media, genre, styles, and forms." (See Walton 1970: 198–99; cf. 338–39 in the original version.) In any case, I think that the genre appearance claim and the genre reality claim are as plausible as the category appearance claim and the category reality claim, whether or not Walton would regard the genre appearance claim and the genre reality claim as instances of the category appearance claim and the category reality claim, respectively.

8 Palliser 1995: 51. In a later chapter, we learn that the manuscript was published in 1958 as *The Throat Surgeon*, which Sholto MacTweed reads as a *roman à clef*. (He thinks that it is about Jack the Ripper.) See Palliser 1995: 175–76. I ignore MacTweed's interpretation in the text.

9 Palliser 1995: 43, 51; italics in original.

10 Palliser 1995: 51. McCoo also suggests "a few minor revisions" to other passages, which describe surgical procedures in language that are "too disgusting to quote" and that "shows a complete misjudgement of what our readers are entitled to expect." See Palliser 1995: 45, 51.

11 Palliser 1995: 43; italics in original.

12 I have transposed considerations about categories into considerations about genres. (See note 7.)

13 Walton 1970: 212.

14 See Walton 1970: 212.

15 Walton is not here endorsing the sentiment. He comes closer to endorsing it later, when he says "I am willing to agree that whether an artist intended his work to be coherent or serene has nothing essentially to do with whether it is coherent or serene." See Walton 1970: 217. To multiply *Donnie Darko* examples, Richard Kelly might have intended the movie to be coherent. But his intending it so does not make it so.

16 "Commentary with Writer/Director Richard Kelly & Jake Gyllenhaal" on the *Donnie Darko* DVD.

17 Quoted in Kohn 2008.

18 Walton 1970: 212.

19 Walton 1970: 199; emphasis in original. It is not clear whether Walton defines standard, variable, and contra-standard features with respect to all categories or merely with respect to perceptually distinguishable categories. See Walton 1970: 198–99. In any case, I think that the distinction between standard, variable, and contra-standard features can be extended to all categories, whether or not Walton intended it to be so.

20 See Walton 1970: 199.

21 Walton 1970: 212.

22 There is also a meta-point to be made here: *Betrayals* appears to be aesthetically better when *The New Surgeon* is perceived in the genre horror. One of the morals of *Betrayals* is that every text betrays itself. In this case, McCoo's report betrays itself by providing evidence about the true nature of *The New Surgeon*.

23 Steven Spielberg, who developed *Artificial Intelligence: A.I.* (2001) with Stanley Kubrick, said, "all the parts of *A.I.* that people assume were Stanley's were mine. And all the parts of *A.I.* that people accuse me of sweetening and softening and sentimentalizing were all Stanley's." Quoted in Leydon 2002; italics in original.

24 Walton (1970: 216 n. 14) suggests that, if a work of art *W* appears to have an aesthetic property F when it is perceived in a category C and it is correct to perceive *W* in C, then *W* really has F – even if *W* does not appear to have F when it is perceived in a category C* and it is correct to perceive *W* in C*. But this suggestion does not help us avoid the contradiction in the case at hand. For "Hush" appears to have one aesthetic property (*being merely somewhat eerie*) when it is perceived in one genre (the genre horror) and it is correct to perceive "Hush" in that genre – even if "Hush" does not appear to have that property when it is perceived in another genre (the genre *teen drama*) and it is correct to perceive "Hush" in that genre. And "Hush" appears to have an apparently incompatible aesthetic property (*being extremely eerie*) when it is perceived in one genre (the genre *teen drama*) and it is correct to perceive "Hush" in that genre – even if "Hush" does not appear to have that property when it is perceived in another genre (the genre horror) and it is correct to perceive "Hush" in that genre. So, on Walton's suggestion, it still follows that "Hush" has apparently incompatible properties. Another, more radical, response is to deny that "Hush"-as-perceived-in-the-genre-horror is identical to "Hush"-as-perceived-in-the-genre-*teen-drama* and to treat the foregoing as an argument for their distinctness. For this sort of response, see Levinson 1980: 68–73.

25 For the sake of the example, I am assuming that the genres horror and *teen drama* are the only components of the hybrid genre *teen horror* (which might, or might not, be the same genre as the genre slasher film). I am no expert on the genre *teen horror*, but I would expect this assumption to be an oversimplification.

26 "Commentary: David Fincher" and "Commentary: David Fincher, Brad Pitt, Edward Norton & Helena Bonham Carter" on the *Fight Club* DVD.

27 Quoted in Sragow 1999.

28 "Commentary: Chuck Palahniuk and Jim Uhls" on the *Fight Club* DVD. Uhls agreed.

29 "Commentary: David Fincher, Brad Pitt, Edward Norton & Helena Bonham Carter."

30 "Commentary: David Fincher, Brad Pitt, Edward Norton & Helena Bonham Carter."

31 "Commentary: David Fincher, Brad Pitt, Edward Norton & Helena Bonham Carter."

32 "Commentary: David Fincher."

33 "Commentary: David Fincher."

34 "Commentary: David Fincher, Brad Pitt, Edward Norton & Helena Bonham Carter."

35 "Commentary: David Fincher, Brad Pitt, Edward Norton & Helena Bonham Carter." Palahniuk also made the comparison to Jerry Lewis. See "Commentary: Chuck Palahniuk and Jim Uhls." Norton made a comparison to Jerry Lewis and Harold Lloyd. See "Commentary: David Fincher, Brad Pitt, Edward Norton & Helena Bonham Carter."

36 "Commentary: David Fincher, Brad Pitt, Edward Norton & Helena Bonham Carter." Fincher and Norton agreed. The detectives are named after Andrew Kevin Walker, who worked on the script but, for reasons having to do with the Writers Guild of America, could not be mentioned in the credits.

37 "Commentary: David Fincher."

38 Quoted in Sragow 1999.

39 "Commentary: David Fincher," "Commentary: David Fincher, Brad Pitt, Edward Norton & Helena Bonham Carter," and "Commentary: Chuck Palahniuk and Jim Uhls."

40 This sort of skepticism is common. It is shared by, for example, Cavell (1981) and Carroll (1982).

41 It is this mismatching of the romantic leads, especially when it is based on race or class, that allows certain films to be vehicles for social criticism. See Wartenberg 1999.

42 In *Bluebeard's Eighth Wife* (1938), it is actually the other way around: a millionaire American businessman, Michael Barndon (Gary Cooper), says, "I just want the tops" and the daughter of a destitute French nobleman, Nicole De Loiselle (Claudette Colbert), who it turns out is shopping for a bargain for her father, says, "I'll buy the trousers. . . . I'm looking for pajamas for a gentleman, and for his purpose the trousers are enough."

43 It might be correct to perceive *Charade* in a hybrid genre such as *romantic comedy thriller*. But that does not mean that *Charade* does not possess features that are standard for the genre *romantic comedy*. It might also be correct to perceive *Charade* simply in the genre *romantic comedy*; and, even if it is correct to perceive *Charade* only in a hybrid genre such as *romantic comedy thriller*, I think that the mistaken identity plot is connected to the *romantic comedy* component of that hybrid genre. At the end of the film, when Regina and Brian end up together,

she says, "Oh, I love you, Adam, Alex, Peter, Brian, whatever your name is. Oh, I love you. I hope we have a lot of boys and we can name them all after you."

44 *Down with Love* is a parody of films like *Pillow Talk* (1959). But that does not mean that *Down with Love* does not possess features that are standard for the genre *romantic comedy*. On the contrary, it possesses features that are standard for the genre *romantic comedy*, but it does so in an exaggerated manner.

45 This key variation on the genre *romantic comedy* also sets *Fight Club* apart from the films that Cavell (1981) has dubbed "comedies of remarriage." In those films, a character struggles to recognize the reality of another. (Here I am following Wartenberg 1999: 39.) In *Fight Club*, by contrast, a character struggles to recognize the unreality of another.

46 *The Incredibly True Adventure of Two Girls in Love* is not part of the canon in the way that the great Nora Ephron romantic comedies from the 1980s and 1990s (*When Harry Met Sally . . .* (1989), *Sleepless in Seattle* (1993), and *You've Got Mail* (1998)) or the great Richard Curtis romantic comedies from the 1990s and 2000s (*Four Weddings and a Funeral* (1994), *Notting Hill* (1999), and *Love Actually* (2003)) are. But I think that, like *Edge of Seventeen* (1998), *The Incredibly True Adventure of Two Girls in Love* is a queer take on the great John Hughes teen romantic comedies from the 1980s: *Sixteen Candles* (1984), *Pretty in Pink* (1986), and *Some Kind of Wonderful* (1987). So I think that *The Incredibly True Adventure of Two Girls in Love* is actually a fairly reliable indicator of what features are standard for the genre *romantic comedy*.

47 *Keeping the Faith* was directed by Edward Norton and written by Stuart Blumberg, who had a small part in *Fight Club*.

48 "Commentary: David Fincher."

49 "Commentary: Chuck Palahniuk and Jim Uhls."

50 "Commentary: Chuck Palahniuk and Jim Uhls."

51 "Commentary: Chuck Palahniuk and Jim Uhls."

52 Quoted in Sragow 1999.

53 Curtis 1999: 13.

54 Curtis 1999: 13.

55 Curtis 1999: 13.

56 Curtis 1999: 17.

57 The descriptions of Sally and Harry come from Ephron 2004: x.

58 Quoted in *How Harry Met Sally . . .* (2000), a documentary included on the 2001 DVD of *When Harry Met Sally. . . .*

59 Quoted in *How Harry Met Sally. . . .*

60 One topic to explore would be the connection between Marla and Audrey Hepburn. Palahniuk described Marla as "Audrey Hepburn on heroin." See "Commentary: Chuck Palahniuk and Jim Uhls."

61 In *The Lady Vanishes* (1938), a British woman who is going home to get married, Iris Henderson (Margaret Lockwock), says to a bow-tied ethnomusicologist who is threatening to share her digs for the night, Gilbert (Michael Redgrave),

"You're the most contemptible person I've ever met in all my life."
"Confidentially, I think you're a bit of a stinker, too," he replies.
62 Harvey 1998: 108.
63 "Commentary: David Fincher."
64 "Commentary: David Fincher, Brad Pitt, Edward Norton & Helena Bonham Carter."
65 "Commentary: David Fincher."
66 For a discussion of some of the narrative tricks that *Fight Club* uses to fool viewers, see Wilson 2006: 91–93 and part I of Wilson and Shpall, this volume.
67 Quoted in *How Harry Met Sally*. . . .
68 In *How Harry Met Sally* . . ., Reiner says that in *When Harry Met Sally* . . . there are no "external obstacles."
69 In *How Harry Met Sally* . . ., Fischer says that the obstacles in *When Harry Met Sally* . . . are "all internal."
70 Quoted in *How Harry Met Sally*. . . .
71 Quoted in Sragow 1999; italics in original.
72 "Commentary: David Fincher."

Works cited

Carroll, N. (1982) Review of Cavell 1981, *Journal of Aesthetics and Art Criticism*, 41: 103–6.

Cavell, S. (1981) *Pursuits of Happiness: The Hollywood Comedy of Remarriage*, Cambridge, MA: Harvard University Press.

Curtis, R. (1999) "A Foreword," in *Notting Hill*, London: Hodder & Stoughton.

Ephron, N. (2004) "Introduction," in *When Harry Met Sally* . . ., New York, NY: Knopf.

Harvey, J. (1998, originally 1987) *Romantic Comedy in Hollywood from Lubitsch to Sturges*, New York, NY: Da Capo.

Kohn, E. (2008) "Interview: M. Night Shyamalan," *Cinematical.com*. Online. Available HTTP: www.cinematical.com/2008/06/10/interview-m-night-shyamalan/ (accessed 22 June 2009).

Levinson, J. (1980) "What a Musical Work Is," *Journal of Philosophy*, 77: 5–28; reprinted in (1990) *Music, Art, and Metaphysics: Essays in Philosophical Aesthetics*, Ithaca, NY: Cornell University Press.

Leydon, J. (2002) "Steven Spielberg and Tom Cruise: Their 'Minority Report' looks at the day after tomorrow—and is relevant to today," *Movingpictureshow.com*. Online. Available HTTP: www.movingpictureshow.com/dialogues/mpsSpielbergCruise.html (accessed 17 June 2009).

Palliser, C. (1995, originally 1994) *Betrayals*, London: Vintage.

Sragow, M. (1999) "Testorama," *Salon.com*. Online. Available HTTP: www.salon.com/ent/col/srag/1999/10/14/fincher/ (accessed 3 June 2009).

Walton, K.L. (1970) "Categories of Art," *Philosophical Review*, 79: 334–67; reprinted in (2008) *Marvelous Images: On Values and the Arts*, Oxford: Oxford University Press.

Wartenberg, T.E. (1999) *Unlikely Couples: Movie Romance as Social Criticism, Thinking Through Cinema,* Boulder, CO: Westview.

Wilson, G. (2006) "Transparency and Twist in Narrative Fiction Film," *Journal of Aesthetics and Art Criticism,* 64: 81–96; reprinted in M. Smith and T.E. Wartenberg (eds) (2006) *Thinking Through Cinema: Film as Philosophy,* London: Blackwell.

Further reading

Walton's "Categories of Art" is a classic. One strand of its influence is visible in ongoing debates about *esthetic empiricism,* which is (roughly) the view that which esthetic properties a work of art has is determined by its perceivable properties. Some have sought to defend a moderate version of esthetic empiricism that is compatible with Walton's examples. See, for example, Dodd, J. (2007) *Works of Music: An Essay in Ontology,* Oxford: Oxford University Press and several of the essays reprinted in Zangwill, N. (2001) *The Metaphysics of Beauty,* Ithaca, NY: Cornell University Press. Others have sought to expand on Walton's examples and use them to argue for a form of *esthetic contextualism,* which is (roughly) the view that which esthetic properties a work of art has is determined, in part, by the art-historical context in which it was produced. See, for example, Currie, G. (1989) *An Ontology of Art,* London: Macmillan; several of the essays reprinted in Levinson's *Music, Art, and Metaphysics;* and Davies, D. (2004) *Art as Performance,* Malden, MA: Blackwell. For a careful discussion of Walton's paper (one that disagrees in various ways with the interpretation offered in this chapter), see Laetz, B. (2010) "Kendall Walton's 'Categories of Art': A Critical Commentary," *British Journal of Aesthetics* 50: 287–306.

Index

Note: page references in *italics* indicate illustrations

Memento

Series: Philosophers on Film

Andrew Kania, Trinity University, USA

'...clear, accessible, and engaging introductions to basic philosophical questions and concepts in a way that enriches our understanding of *Memento* and philosophy both. . . The range of topics, the dialogue the essays themselves foster, and the genuine philosophical light shed by them will, as Hanley says, not only "get you thinking" but "keep you thinking." This collection is a good choice for undergraduate courses in philosophy and is accessible enough to be of interest to philosophically minded fans of *Memento* or film more generally.' - *Metapsychology*

This is the first book to explore and address the myriad philosophical questions raised by the film, concerning personal identity, free will, memory, knowledge, and action. It also explores problems in aesthetics raised by the film through its narrative structure, ontology, and genre. Beginning with a helpful introduction that places the film in context and maps out its complex structure, specially commissioned chapters examine the following topics:

- memory, emotion, and self-consciousness
- agency, free will, and responsibility
- personal identity
- narrative and popular cinema
- the film genre of neo-noir
- *Memento* and multimedia

Including annotated further reading at the end of each chapter, *Memento* is essential reading for students interested in philosophy and film studies.

Pb: 978-0-415-77474-1
216 x 138 : 192pp

For more information and to order a copy visit
www.routledge.com/9780415774741

Available from all good bookshops

Lightning Source UK Ltd.
Milton Keynes UK
UKOW01f2256120815

256807UK00015B/224/P